Human Evidence in Criminal Justice

Second Edition

Larry Miller
William Bass
Ramona Miller

Pilgrimage

CJ Criminal Justice Studies
Anderson Publishing Co./Cincinnati, Ohio

HUMAN EVIDENCE IN CRIMINAL JUSTICE

ISBN: 0-932930-68-9

Second Edition

Cover design by Keith Rutherford

ACKNOWLEDGEMENTS

Many professional colleagues in academic and agency settings provided valuable input regarding the development of this book. Of special mention are A.M. Brown, Director of Walters State Community College Crime Laboratory; and Nicholas J. Carimi, Director of Forensic Sciences Services at East Tennessee State University.

We are especially indebted to Teresa Taylor for her illustrations and artwork.

Finally, we wish to thank Brenda Blankenship for her typing and editorial assistance.

CONTENTS

PREFACE

Human evidence is that evidence associated with the identification of individuals, living or dead, for legal purposes. Human evidence is one of the more important aspects of the criminal investigation process. Identification of suspects of crimes, as well as deceased individuals, constitutes a major function of law enforcement and forensic medical personnel. Traditionally, law enforcement officers have concentrated on the identification of criminal suspects and have relegated the more complicated task of identifying deceased individuals to medical personnel. Much has been written concerning the human evidence dimension of identifying suspects of crimes. Nearly all criminal investigation texts include a substantial amount of information regarding identification of living individuals. However, few texts in the law enforcement field detail the methods employed to identify deceased human bodies. It is essential that the law enforcement officer be familiar with human evidence for living and deceased individuals.

This book is designed to give the reader a basic understanding of the processes of human evidence relating to the field of law enforcement. It is not intended to make a human evidence/identification expert of the reader, but to expose the reader to the techniques utilized in human evidence. Consequently, this should serve to familiarize the reader with available information and sources of more detailed information.

This book was written primarily for the student and practitioner in law enforcement fields. However, students and practitioners in the fields of forensic medicine, forensic anthropology, forensic odontology, and criminalistics may also find this book useful and informative.

FOREWORD

Human Evidence provides information that is vital to the criminal investigator. The authors present information that every detective who is investigating crimes committed against humans must know.

Far too many investigators rely on confessions as the main support for their case. Sometimes this reliance on a confession is because the investigator is either unskilled in the gathering of physical evidence or lacks knowledge of its possible uses. Confessions can be challenged in court and eye witness accounts are sometimes suspect or conflicting, but physical evidence, when legally obtained, is less open to challenge. The loss of a burglary case because of improper handling of evidence is a problem, but the loss of a homicide case because of improper handling is tragic.

Analysis and comparison techniques are ever changing and improving. No book can keep up with the newest methods available. Human Evidence is no exception, but this book does provide information that is current at the time of publication.

Human Evidence provides the reader with current information that is clear, concise and easy to understand. Reading this book will help students understand what detectives do to solve crimes. Detectives will learn about new methods and techniques.

Hal Nees
Chief, Detective Division
Boulder, Colorado Police

1

INTRODUCTION TO HUMAN EVIDENCE

I. Human Evidence Defined

When the term "human evidence" comes to mind, a variety of related topics may emerge. Criminal investigators may think of human evidence as documentary, physical, or testimonial evidence produced through interviews, interrogations and crime scene searches. Attorneys may envision human evidence as testimonial evidence from a witness in court. Crime laboratory and forensic medical persons may define human evidence as physical evidence produced through laboratory analyses and autopsies.

The dimensions of human evidence are multi-faceted. One may define human evidence as that physical evidence produced directly from the human body which allows law enforcement officials, forensic scientists, and legal professionals to identify an individual with a certain degree of probability. Human evidence, in the most basic form and dimension, is human identification in a legal application. Those forms of physical evidence produced directly through the human body include 1) fingerprint identification; 2) body fluid evidence (serology); 3) human hair identification; 4) voiceprints; 5) skin prints (ears, lips, etc.); 6) handwriting; 7) post-mortem identification (autopsies); and 8) anthropology and selected identification. Each topic involves the identification of a human individual in relation to legal evidence.

For some time, the law enforcement and scientific communities have searched for a positive method to identify a particular individual biologically. Individuals are unique, but this uniqueness can only be "proven" by statistical probability. There is no current form of human biological identification evidence that can be defined as 100 percent positive. Fingerprints have been accepted as a "positive" form of human evidence in courts. However, even fingerprints cannot be defined as a positive form of human evidence. How can one be sure that two individuals do not have the same set of fingerprints? Statistically speaking, the probability of two individuals possessing the same fingerprint is 64 billion to one (1:154). Given the current world population of approximately 4 billion, fingerprints become a very viable form of circumstantial evidence . Although the laws of probability refute this, a future instance may arise whereby two individuals possess the same set of fingerprints. Consequently, all forms of human evidence are related to statistical probability and tied to individual uniqueness. All human evidence is considered technically as circumstantial evidence. No human evidence expert can say that he/she is 100 percent positive based on the uniqueness of an individual, regardless of the form of evidence produced (e.g., fingerprints, blood, hair, etc.).

II. Early Forms Of Human Identification

Generally, early identification of individuals was to denote the membership in a particular group. Individuals were identified as members of certain tribes, classes, clans, castes, or families. The methods of identification consisted of particular modes of dress, mutilation markings, or tatoos. Criminals were often marked by branding or mutilation for future identification purposes.

Description has always played an important role in the human identification process. It was on vocal description that most early processes of human identification were based. The basic requirement was the ability to observe and to pass the observation on to others in the form of a word picture.

Systematic forms of human identification did not appear until the late 19th century. Physical anthropologists played an important role in the development of systematic methods of human identification. Their research into the biological differences of man provided law enforcement with many human identification methods including fingerprints, body measurements, portrait parle', and skeletal identification.

III. Cesare Lombroso

Cesare Lombroso (1835-1909) was one of the first physical anthropologists to develop a criminal identification theory based upon human body characteristics. In 1876, Lombroso first published his "Born Criminal" theory in a pamphlet and later published a three volume book on the subject (2). Lombroso based much of his theory on physical measurements (anthropometry) of individuals taken at a prison asylum in Pavia, Italy. Lombroso stated that criminals were by birth a distinct type that could be identified by certain physical anomalies. Physical anomalies in criminals included such characteristics as asymmetrical craniums, long lower jaws, flattened noses, and scanty beards. Lombroso contended that their physical anomalies did not cause crime, but identified the personality of the individual predisposed to criminal behavior. He concluded that the personality of these individuals was a regression to the savage type of man -- an atavism -- or a product of degeneration. Many cartoons and caricatures today still portray the criminal with these physical characteristics.

IV. Alphonse Bertillon

During the same period that Lombroso published his "Born Criminal" theory, Alphonse Bertillon developed the first widely accepted systematic method of human identification for law enforcement.

Bertillon commanded the police identification section in Paris during the 1800's. An amateur physical anthropologist, Bertillon devised an identification system that incorporated anthropometry. The Bertillon identification system was composed of four items: 1) a full face and profile photograph of the subject; 2) a detailed, precise description; 3) fingerprints; and, 4) anthropometric measurements of the subject.

Although Bertillon used fingerprints as an auxiliary system and even "broke" a number of cases using fingerprints, he maintained that anthropometric measurements was a more accurate method of identification. The anthropometric measurements included: 1) length of the arms; 2) sitting height; and, 3) caliper measurements of the head, right arm, left foot, left middle finger, left little finger, left forearm, and right ear.

Many countries, including the United States, adopted the Bertillon system of anthropometry for law enforcement and prison use. After a relatively short time, however, certain shortcomings of the Bertillon system became evident. Problems with the Bertillon system were often due to measurement precision (individual clerk recording variations) and changes in the body due to the growth and/or maturing process.

The decline and final end of the Bertillon system was marked by the Will West - William West case of 1903. During the processing of Will West at the Federal prison in Leavenworth, Kansas, a technician insisted that West had been there previously. Further investigation revealed William West who was already a prisoner at Leavenworth serving a life sentence for murder. The two prisoners were virtually identical in all physical respects. A comparison of fingerprints showed no similarity, however. Will and William West were unknown to one another and no relationship could be established between the two.

V. Emergence Of Fingerprint
Identification

After the Will West - William West case, law enforcement agencies and prison systems began turning to the use of fingerprints for human identification purposes. Fingerprints had been studied by numerous physical anthropologists several years prior to its acceptance in the law enforcement field.

The Chinese seem to have been the predicators of the conception of the uniqueness of finger, palm, and footprints. A 12th century novel by Shi-Naignan, The Story of the River , recounted the use of the sole and palm prints for sealing the sale of children into slavery.

One of the first systematic methods of classifying fingerprints for law enforcement purposes was developed by Sir Edward R. Henry (3). Henry, impressed with the works of physical anthropologists in the area of fingerprint identification, developed a classification system for fingerprints in 1900. In 1901, Henry was appointed assistant commissioner at Scotland Yard and encouraged the adoption of his fingerprint identification system. By 1914, fingerprints as a system of human identification became worldwide, with the Henry system of classification becoming standard in most countries.

When J. Edgar Hoover was appointed Director of the Federal Bureau of Investigation in 1924, he established the FBI's Identification Bureau with 800,000 fingerprints on file. Today, the FBI has over two million fingerprints on file.

VI. Anthropometry

Although anthropometry as a primary system of human identification has been replaced by

5

fingerprints in the law enforcement field, it still has some merit in criminal investigations. In many crimes the perpetrator leaves articles of clothing or traces of shoeprints at the crime scene. Measurements taken of shoeprints and the sizes of articles of clothing, such as gloves or hats, may indicate the perpetrator's size, weight, and height. The amount of wear on a shoe sole may also indicate the gait of a person. Often times these items may be the only source of information for identification purposes, and in this light, anthropometry is an important tool of the investigator.

VII. Portrait Parle'

The systematic method of making detailed written and verbal description of the human body for identification purposes is known as portrait parle'. Portrait parle' is based on The Bertillon System of human identification. The following outline consists of the basic information required for portrait parle':

I. General Impression
  A. Type of Individuals
     1. Personality
     2. Social status
  B. Comparison with other well-known individuals (i.e. actors or political figures).

II. Age and Sex

III. Race or Color
  A. Caucasoid - White
  B. Negroid - Black
  C. Mongoloid - Red or Yellow

IV. Body Type
  A. Height - estimated within 2 inches
  B. Weight - estimated within 5 pounds
  C. Build - thin, slender, medium, stout
  D. Posture - erect, slouching, round-shouldered; carriage

V. Dress
   A.   Clothing worn-type, condition, color
   B.   Jewelry
   C.   Shoes

VI. Head (see Figure 1)
   A.   Shape - round, flat, bulging,
        eggshaped; crown
   B.   Profile - forehead, nose type,
        mouth, chin
   C.   Face - general impression followed
        by description of features
        1.   Eyebrows, mustache,
             beard, sideburns
        2.   Eyes - small, medium, large;
             color; glasses
        3.   Ears - size, shape, angle
        4.   Cheeks - high, low, prominent,
             sunken, medium
        5.   Nose - size and shape
        6.   Mouth - wide, small; general
             expression
        7.   Teeth - shade, condition
        8.   Chin - size, shape; general
             impression
        9.   Jaw - length, shape, lean,
             heavy, medium

VII. Torso
   A.   Shoulders - width and shape
   B.   Chest - width and thickness
   C.   Waist - size, stomach shape

VIII. Extremities
   A.   Arms and hands - length,
        size, hair, condition, nails
   B.   Legs and feet - length, shape, size

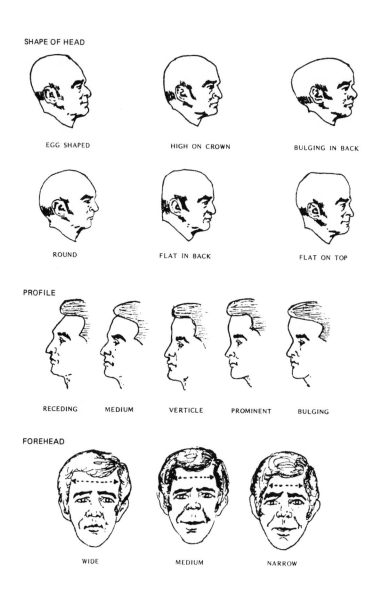

SHAPE OF HEAD

EGG SHAPED   HIGH ON CROWN   BULGING IN BACK

ROUND   FLAT IN BACK   FLAT ON TOP

PROFILE

RECEDING   MEDIUM   VERTICLE   PROMINENT   BULGING

FOREHEAD

WIDE   MEDIUM   NARROW

FIGURE 1a. PORTRAIT PARLE'.

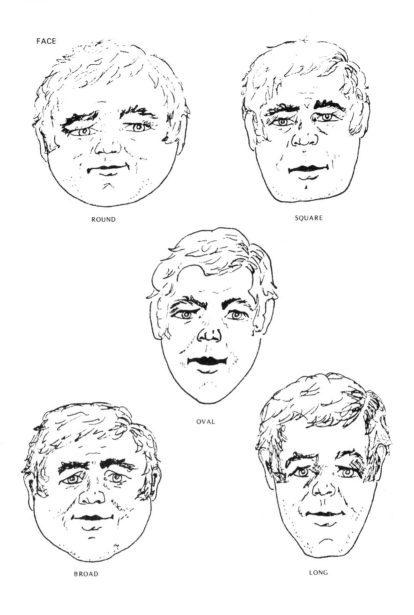

FACE

ROUND

SQUARE

OVAL

BROAD

LONG

FIGURE 1b. PORTRAIT PARLE'.

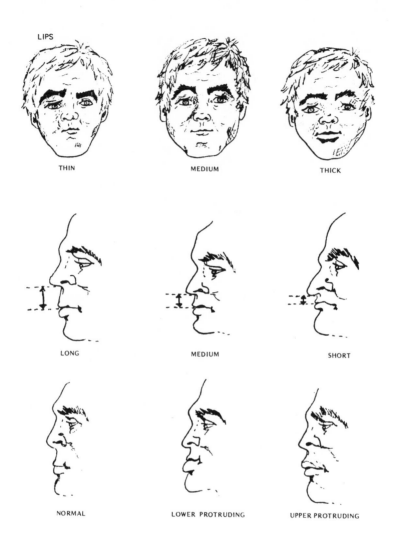

LIPS

THIN   MEDIUM   THICK

LONG   MEDIUM   SHORT

NORMAL   LOWER PROTRUDING   UPPER PROTRUDING

FIGURE 1c. PORTRAIT PARLE'.

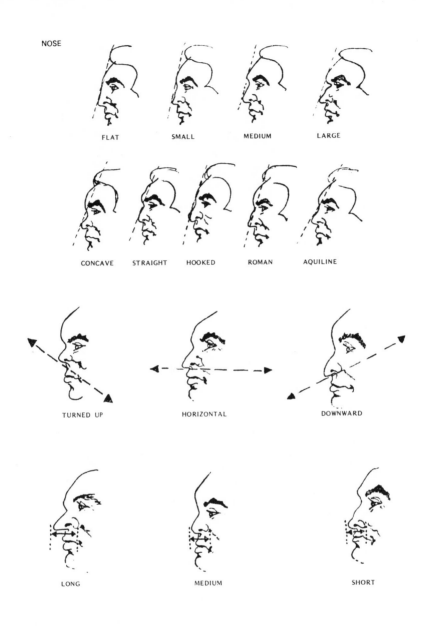

NOSE

FLAT   SMALL   MEDIUM   LARGE

CONCAVE   STRAIGHT   HOOKED   ROMAN   AQUILINE

TURNED UP   HORIZONTAL   DOWNWARD

LONG   MEDIUM   SHORT

FIGURE 1d. PORTRAIT PARLE'.

11

NOSE

NARROW MEDIUM WIDE

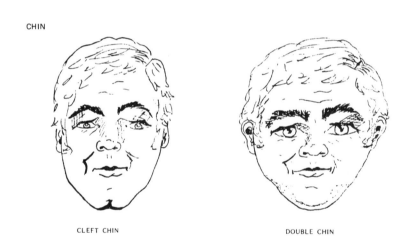

CHIN

CLEFT CHIN DOUBLE CHIN

FIGURE 1e. PORTRAIT PARLE'.

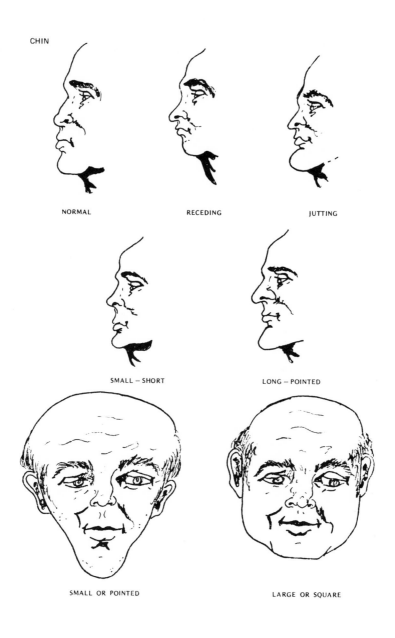

CHIN

NORMAL   RECEDING   JUTTING

SMALL – SHORT   LONG – POINTED

SMALL OR POINTED   LARGE OR SQUARE

FIGURE 1f.   PORTRAIT PARLE'.

13

EARS

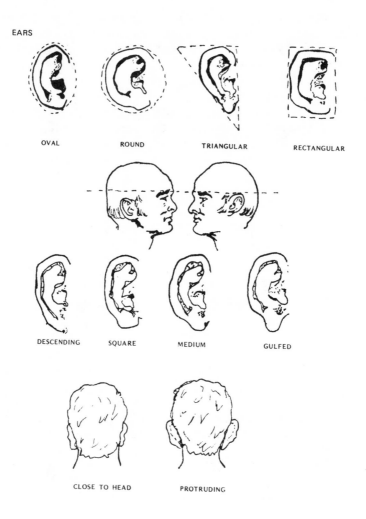

OVAL   ROUND   TRIANGULAR   RECTANGULAR

DESCENDING   SQUARE   MEDIUM   GULFED

CLOSE TO HEAD   PROTRUDING

FIGURE 1g. PORTRAIT PARLE'.

14

VIII. Composites

The oldest method of producing pictures is from verbal descriptions or artist composite. Artists who can accurately produce a drawing from a witness' description are quite rare. Most law enforcement agencies do not have such a skilled artist available nor the budget capable of affording one. However, for the law enforcement agency fortunate enough to have such a skilled artist avialable, the following steps are outlined as a guide for an artist's composition:

1. <u>Separate witnesses</u> - if more than one witness can identify an individual, it is best to separate them so that one witness' description may not be impressed on the other witnesses.'

2. <u>Portrait Parle'</u> - witnesses should be asked to write down the physical description of the individual after initial interview. Portrait parle' is especially helpful in this step.

3. <u>Compare Descriptions</u> - the investigator should compare the written descriptions of the witnesses in order to obtain common features of the individual.

4. <u>Primary Sketch</u> - the composite artist should now begin the sketch based upon the common feature descriptions. Witnesses should be called in separately to examine the sketches and suggest improvements or alterations.

5. <u>Final Sketch</u> - the composite artist uses the improvements to finalize the sketch. Witnesses should now be asked as a group to examine the sketch and make any minor improvements (see Figure 2).

In the 1960's, commercially prepared composite "kits" became available to law enforcement agencies. These composite kits

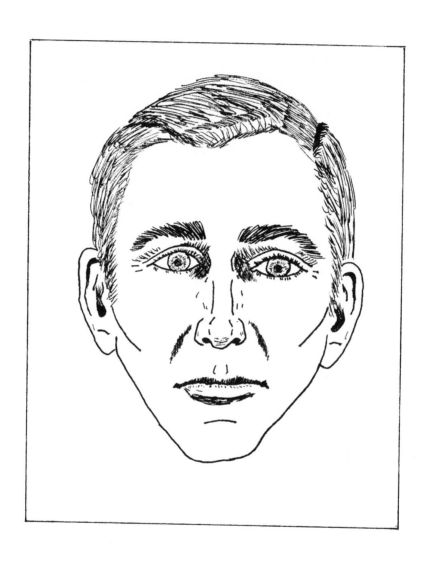

FIGURE 2.   EXAMPLE OF A COMPOSITE DRAWING.

16

contain numerous fact forms and features that can be arranged into thousands of different faces. There are several composite kits presently available commercially to law enforcement agencies. The more common kits contain plastic transparent sheets with a single feature (i.e., eyes, nose, mouth, hair, etc.) either drawn or photographed on each sheet. The plastic sheets are sequentially overlayed in order to create a resemblance of a described individual.

The use of composite kits follow the same steps as outlined for an artist composite. These composite kits are generally more economical and therefore more readily available to law enforcement agencies than composite artists. It should be noted that no composite, whether an artists' rendering or kit composite, can produce an identical likeness of an individual.

IX. Photography

Photographs are the best means of visually identifying an individual. Identification photographs of criminals (mug shots) have been used since the mid 1800's when the photographic process was first developed. Early mug shots consisted of the full face of the criminal suspect. Bertillon began using full face and profile photographs in his identification system.

Today, most law enforcement agencies photograph suspects as a routine-procedure in the "booking" process. While black and white mug shots are still very common among law enforcement agencies, the use of color photographs presents more detail to complexions and provides a more vivid and realistic detailed description of an individual. Generally, law enforcement agencies include a height scale in mug shots so that the height of the individual can be recorded on the photograph. Unfortunately, many of these height scales provide inaccurate measurements due to camera angles, shoes worn by the individual, etc.

17

Photographs, such as mug shots, can also be used for line-up purposes. Many law enforcement agencies do not have the facilities to provide for witness identification at line-ups. Increasingly, photographic line-ups are being used by law enforcement agencies. A further discussion of photographic line-ups is included in Chapter 9.

References

1. Cummins, H. and Midlo, C. Finger Prints, Palms and Soles , (New York: Dover Publications, Inc., 1961), p. 154.

2. Lombroso, Cesare, L'uomo delinquente , (Torino, Italy: Bocca, 1896-97).

3. Henry, Edward R., Classification and Uses of Finger Prints , 8th Edition, (London: H. M. Stationery Office, 1937).

Additional Reading

Allison, Harrison C., Personal Identification , (Boston: Holbrook Press, 1973).

Department of the Army, Criminal Investigation, FM 1920 , (Washington, D.C.: Government Printing Office, 1951).

Galton, Sir Francis, Finger Prints , (New York: DeCapo Press, 1965).

Hopper, W.R., "Photo-Fit: The Penry Facial Identification Technique," Journal of Forensic Science Society , 13:77, 1973.

Lombroso-Ferrero, Gina, Criminal Man, According to the Classification of Cesare Lombroso , (New York: G.P. Putman and Sons, 1911).

Nash, Donald J., et al. Individual Identification and the Law Enforcement Officer (Springfield, Illinois: Charles C. Thomas, 1978).

O'Hara, Charles E., Fundamentals of Criminal Investigation , 5th Edition, (Springfield, Illinois: Charles C. Thomas, 1980).

Owens, C., "Identi-Kit Enters its Second Decade, Ever Growing at Home and Abroad," Finger Print and Identification Magazine , November 3-17, 1970.

Penri, J., Looking at Faces and Remembering Them , (London: Elek Books, 1971).

Sansone, S.J., Police Photography , (Cincinnati: W.H. Anderson Publishing, 1977).

Zavola, A. and Paley, J.J. (Eds.), Personal Appearance Identification , (Springfield, Illinois: Charles C. Thomas, 1972).

2

FINGERPRINTS

I. Fingerprints As Human Evidence

Fingerprints are one of the most common and valuable forms of evidence for human identification. It is routine procedure for law enforcement officers to search for fingerprints left at the scene of a crime in order that they may identify the perpetrator. It is also routine for law enforcement and correction agencies to fingerprint arrested and convicted offenders. The courts recognize that fingerprint identification is one of the surest methods of identification known. The primary purpose of fingerprinting is to "positively" identify an individual. Another purpose of fingerprinting is to provide evidence of association; such as the comparison of fingerprints of a criminally accused individual with fingerprints left at the scene of a crime.

II. Anatomy of Fingerprints

Physical anthropologists have studied fingerprint variation in individuals for decades. Anthropologists typically use the terms dactylography or dermatoglyphics when referring to fingerprints and footprints. The term dactylography comes from the Greek words for finger (daktylos) and to write (graphein). Cummins and Midlo formulated the term dermatoglyphics from derma (the skin) and glyphe (to carve) (1).

The skin of humans and other primates exhibits formations of ridges on the palms of the hands, soles of the feet, fingers, and toes. These ridge formations act as a non-skid surface for grasping and clinging. The raised portions on the skin surface are known as friction ridges.

Friction ridges develop during the third and fourth months of human fetal life. At first, they appear as dots built around sweat pores. With time, these dots fuse and enlarge to make up the final fully developed ridge formation. The human being is born with a set of fingerprints that is relatively unchanged throughout the remainder of life.

The human skin is made up of two divisions: 1) the outer epidermis and 2) the underlying layer known as the dermis. Beneath this tissue are glandular tissues, nerve endings, and fat. There are no oil glands in friction ridge skin areas. However, there are sweat glands which secrete perspiration through pores on the friction ridges of the skin (see Figure 3).

Some individuals have attempted to remove their fingerprints by cutting or using acid. Superficial wounds that do not pass through the dermis layer of the skin will not have a lasting effect on the fingerprint formation. Wounds that do not pass through the dermis may leave a permanent scar. Scars will seldom prevent the correct classification of a fingerprint, however. The shape of the friction ridges is controlled by the underlying tissues in the dermis. Therefore, a fingerprint would be difficult to alter by mutilation. Skin grafts of fingerprints have also been used by the criminal community. Such grafts can be identified through variations of pores of the original and the "copy".

The individuality of fingerprints is the most important aspect for human identification. Even identical twins have variations in their fingerprint patterns. To date, there are no two fingerprints known to exist that are duplicates unless they come from the same individual.

Fingerprints do vary in types among individuals. Anthropologists have been somewhat successful in determining the sex, race, and even occupations of persons by analyzing their

22

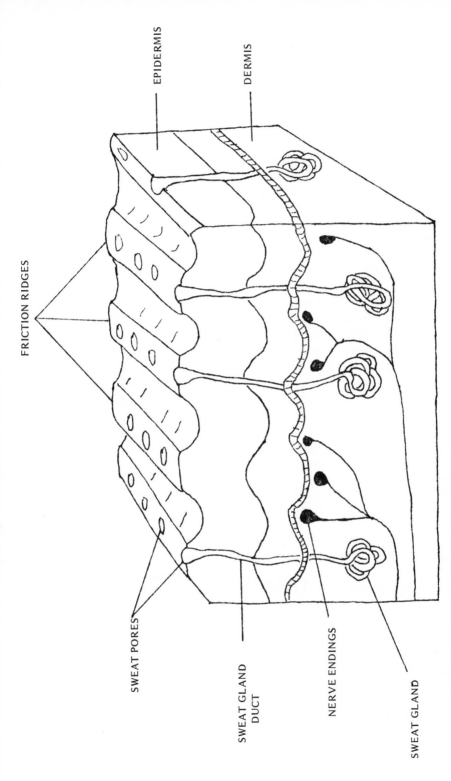

FRICTION RIDGES

EPIDERMIS

DERMIS

SWEAT PORES

SWEAT GLAND DUCT

NERVE ENDINGS

SWEAT GLAND

FIGURE 3. THE STRUCTURE OF RIDGED SKIN.

23

fingerprint characteristics (2: 171-176). Such characteristic variations have not been accepted as a form of positive identification, but can be useful when seeking an individual in criminal investigations.

III. Latent Fingerprints

Fingerprints, as well as palm and sole prints, are composed of raised areas on the skin surface known as friction ridges. These ridges are arranged in a combination of shapes or patterns. The pores within these friction ridges secrete perspiration, salt, and amino acids. When a person touches an object, the greasy residue of the fingerprint remains on the object surface. On most surfaces, these fingerprints are difficult to see. Latent means hidden from view, and latent fingerprints must be developed before they can be seen. Depending upon the techniques of developing latent prints and the degree of skill the investigator possesses, latent fingerprints can be developed from most any surface. Surfaces which are difficult to develop latent prints from include unfinished wood, grained leather, coarse cloth, and other rough surfaces. Time and environmental conditions may also affect the latent print to the extent that the print will be worthless even if developed.

There are two types of latent prints that may be found at the scene of a crime: 1) visible "latent" prints requiring no treatment and 2) latent prints requiring development.

Visible "latent" prints are the type found in blood, paint, wax, or plastic materials. In these cases the friction ridges of the skin will be seen as valleys on the material. It is important to remember this when comparing with inked fingerprints. These prints should only be photographed and noted by location on a crime scene sketch.

Latent prints requiring development can be found by using lighting held at an angle to a surface suspected of having fingerprint evidence. Ultraviolet and infrared lighting may be of help in locating such prints. A recently developed method for locating latent fingerprints is the laser luminescence technique (3: 106-115). This technique involves the use of the argon-ion laser light which excites deposits found in latent fingerprints causing them to luminesce. Once located, latent prints may be developed with fingerprint powders or chemicals.

Development of Latent Fingerprints

The most common method of fingerprint development is with the use of fingerprint powders. Fingerprint powders are fine graphite-like material which adhere to the greasy residue left by friction ridges on non-absorbent surfaces (i.e., glass, finished wood, etc.). Fingerprint powders are available in a variety of colors for use on different contrast surfaces. The powder is usually applied to a surface suspected of bearing a latent print by the use of a brush, or a magnetic wand if the powder is magnetic. The procedure is as follows:

1. Carefully dip the fingerprint brush into the fingerprint powder and sprinkle over the area to be "dusted." Only a small amount of powder is necessary.

2. Lightly brush the powder over the surface until the latent print begins to become visible.

3. Lightly brush away excess powder from the latent print and from between the ridges. Photograph the print before lifting with lifting tape.

4. Take a piece of transparent fingerprint lifting tape and place the tape over the

latent print. Care should be taken not to wrinkle the tape or create bubbles.

5. Lift the tape from the surface and the latent print will adhere to the tape. Place the tape onto a white index card in the same manner as when placing the tape over the latent print.

6. Label the card with the location the print was found, date, time, case, and investigator's name.

Chemical development of latent fingerprints generally involves one or more of four techniques:

1. Iodine Fuming Technique

2. Ninhydrin Technique

3. Silver Nitrate Technique

4. Cyanoacrylate Technique

Chemical development is used for absorbent surfaces such as paper and unfinished wood where fingerprint powders would be useless.

The iodine fuming technique involves the use of iodine crystals. When iodine crystals are subjected to a slight amount of heat, they vaporize rapidly producing violet colored fumes. These fumes are absorbed by fatty or oily matter to which they come in contact. Latent fingerprints on paper or similar material contain fatty or oil residues left by friction ridges. The iodine fumes will be absorbed into these latent prints causing a visible yellowish-brown colored image of the fingerprint to develop. The image is not permanent and must be photographed for future comparison purposes. Iodine fuming may be accomplished by the use a fuming cabinet or by a hand-held glass fuming "gun".

The ninhydrin technique reacts to traces of amino acids (contained in perspiration) that may be present in latent fingerprints. Ninhydrin is a liquid solution which may be brushed or sprayed onto a surface suspected of bearing latent fingerprints. After the surface is sprayed or brushed with ninhydrin, latent prints will begin to develop at room temperature within one to two hours. Ninhydrin developed prints are not permanent as they will begin to loose contrast after a period of time. Photographs must be taken for future comparison purposes.

The silver nitrate technique reacts to the amount of sodium chloride (salt) that may be contained in a latent print from perspiration residues. A developing tray is filled with silver nitrate solution and the surface to be developed is immersed into the tray. Once the latent print becomes visible, the surface is allowed to dry. The time for development is dependent upon the amount of light to which the latent print has been exposed. Sometimes it is best to expose the surface to a bright light before using silver nitrate. Silver nitrate developed prints are also temporary and require that photographs be taken. It should be remembered that silver nitrate will wash away fats, oils, and amino acids; therefore, iodine fuming and/or ninhydrin techniques should be used before the silver nitrate technique.

A recent method of latent fingerprint development, similar in procedure to iodine fuming, is commonly referred to as the "super glue" method (4). The "super glue" method involves a major ingredient in the wide variety of "super glue" products on the market: cyanoacrylate ester. When heated, cyanoacrylate produces fumes which absorb into and crystallize amino acids left by fingerprints. The cyanoacrylate method is particularly useful on articles that are difficult to develop with other fingerprint development methods (e.g., plastic bags, leather, skin, wet surfaces, fabrics, etc.). Cyanoacrylate may be heated directly (approximately 150 degrees F.) or chemically (with sodium hydroxide) to produce the fumes. An iodine fuming cabinet or common cardboard box works quite well with the cyanoacrylate method. The crystallized images of fingerprints appear white and are permanent. For contrast, magnetic fingerprint powder may be used on the crystallized images.

IV. Inked Fingerprints

When a finger is inked and rolled onto a white card, the ink from the friction ridges adheres to the paper, leaving a negative reproduction of the ridge lines reported by white lines indicating the valleys or depressions between the ridges. The basic procedure of taking inked fingerprints is standard among law enforcement agencies. All ten fingers are inked and rolled onto a standardized fingerprint card which includes descriptive data of the subject and, usually, a mug shot of the subject (see Figure 4). The procedure appears to be simple but, unfortunately, many law enforcement officers carelessly fail to master the technique.

1. <u>Equipment Required.</u> The necessary equipment required for taking inked fingerprint impressions consists of a rubber roller, a tube of printer's ink, a slab of glass, a card holder, and a fingerprint card.

2. <u>Inking the Slab.</u> Squeeze four small blobs of printer's ink onto a glass plate (or other nonporous slab) and spread the ink evenly by rolling the rubber roller back and forth.

3. <u>Rolling the Prints.</u> Clean the subject's fingers. The operator must control the rolling process. The fingers should be relaxed for smooth rolling and even pressure. The operator should ink and roll each finger separately, placing the finger so that it is inked from below the first joint to a point as close as possible to the tip, and from nail edge to nail edge.

28

LEAVE BLANK

TYPE OR PRINT ALL INFORMATION IN BLACK

FBI LEAVE BLANK

LAST NAME NAM   FIRST NAME   MIDDLE NAME

STATE USAGE

ALIASES

CONTRIBUTOR
ORI

SIGNATURE OF PERSON FINGERPRINTED

DATE OF BIRTH DOB
Month   Day   Year

THIS DATA MAY BE COMPUTERIZED IN LOCAL, STATE AND NATIONAL FILES

DATE | SIGNATURE OF OFFICIAL TAKING FINGERPRINTS

DATE ARRESTED OR RECEIVED DOA

SEX | RACE | HGT. | WGT. | EYES | HAIR | PLACE OF BIRTH POB

CHARGE

YOUR NO. OCA

LEAVE BLANK

FBI NO. FBI

CLASS.

SID NO. SID

REF.

FINAL DISPOSITION

SOCIAL SECURITY NO. SOC

NCIC CLASS FPC

CAUTION

1. RIGHT THUMB | 2. RIGHT INDEX | 3. RIGHT MIDDLE | 4. RIGHT RING | 5. RIGHT LITTLE

6. LEFT THUMB | 7. LEFT INDEX | 8. LEFT MIDDLE | 9. LEFT RING | 10. LEFT LITTLE

LEFT FOUR FINGERS TAKEN SIMULTANEOUSLY | LEFT THUMB | RIGHT THUMB | RIGHT FOUR FINGERS TAKEN SIMULTANEOUSLY

FIGURE 4. FINGERPRINT CARD.

V. Sole And Palm Prints

The soles of the feet and palms of the hands also consist of friction ridges of individual characters. Prints from both the sole and the palm can be used for identification purposes. With the exception of hospital recording of infants' footprints, there is no systematic record keeping of sole and palm prints. Generally, sole and palm prints are sought at a crime scene as latent prints for comparison with a suspect.

Most hospitals record newborn infants' footprints for identification purposes. Although these footprints can be compared with the adult years later, hospitals are notorious for improper printing procedures, record keeping, and inadequate systems for future record searches. Therefore, identifying an unknown person from hospital footprint records may be nearly impossible.

VI. Fingerprint Pattern Types

There are three basic fingerprint pattern types which can be further divided into eight sub-types (see Figure 5 and 6):

I. Arches
  A. Plain Arch
  B. Tented Arch

II. Loops
  A. Radial loop (curves toward thumb)
  B. Ulna loop (curves away from thumb)

III. Whorls
  A. Plain whorl
  B. Central pocket loop
  C. Double loop
  D. Accidental whorl

In comparing a known set of fingerprints with fingerprints of an unknown source, investigators and crime lab technicians base their examinations

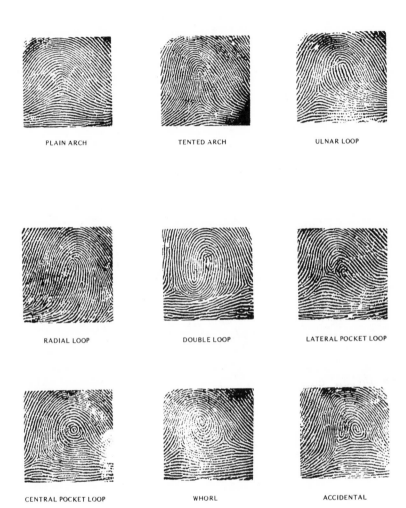

PLAIN ARCH · TENTED ARCH · ULNAR LOOP

RADIAL LOOP · DOUBLE LOOP · LATERAL POCKET LOOP

CENTRAL POCKET LOOP · WHORL · ACCIDENTAL

FIGURE 5.   FINGERPRINT PATTERNS.

31

PLAIN ARCH: RIDGES ENTER UPON ONE SIDE , MAKE A RISE OR CURVE IN CENTER AND FLOW OUT ON OPPOSITE SIDE WITHOUT FORMING AN ANGLE OR AN UPTHRUST.

TENTED ARCH: POSSESSES EITHER AN ANGLE, UPTHRUST, OR LOOP WITHOUT A DELTA.

LOOP: ONE OR MORE RIDGES ENTER ON ONE SIDE, RECURVE, FORM A DELTA AND PASS OUT ON THE SAME SIDE AS WAS ENTERED.

PLAIN WHORL: ONE OR MORE RIDGES MAKE A COMPLETE CIRCUIT, WITH TWO DELTAS, BETWEEN WHICH, WHEN AN IMAGINARY LINE IS DRAWN, AT LEAST ONE RECURVING LINE IS CUT OR TOUCHED.

CENTRAL POCKET LOOP: AT LEAST ONE RECURVING RIDGE, OR AN OBSTRUCTION AT RIGHT ANGLES TO THE LINE OF FLOW, WITH TWO DELTAS, BETWEEN WHICH, WHEN AN IMAGINARY LINE IS DRAWN, NO RECURV--ING LINE IS TOUCHED.

DOUBLE LOOP: CONSISTS OF TWO SEPARATE LOOP FORMATIONS, WITH TWO DELTAS AND TWO DISTINCT SETS OF SHOULDERS. ALSO CALLED TWINNED LOOP.

ACCIDENTAL: COMBINATION OF DIFFERENT PATTERN TYPES WITH THE EXCEPTION OF THE PLAIN ARCH, WITH TWO OR MORE DELTAS, OR A PATTERN WHICH CONFORMS TO NONE OF THE DEFINITIONS OF A PATTERN.

FIGURE 6. FINGERPRINT PATTERN RULES.

on the finer details of the fingerprint pattern. After verifying that the known fingerprint is the same pattern type as the questioned fingerprint, the friction ridges are compared with respect to ridge details. There are ten basic ridge details:

1. <u>Ridge Ending</u> - point at which a friction ridge ends or begins.

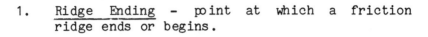

2. <u>Bifurcation or Forked Ridge</u> - a friction ridge that "forks" from one into two ridges.

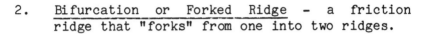

3. <u>Dot or Fragment</u> - a very small portion of a friction ridge.

4. <u>Short Ridge</u> - small portion of a friction ridge.

5. <u>Island or Eye</u> - a single friction ridge bifurcates then converges to make a single ridge.

6. <u>Bridge</u> - a ridge bifurcates and connects to another ridge.

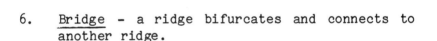

7. <u>Hook or Spur</u> - a ridge bifurcates and appears as a spur or hook.

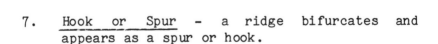

8. <u>Double Bifurcation</u> - two bifurcations from the same ridge.

33

9. <u>Delta</u> - ridges coming to a flow around a short ridge - resembling a triangle.

10. <u>Trifurcation</u> - three ridges emerging from the same point of a single ridge.

The same details can be found on foot and palm prints as well.

When used as evidence in a court of law, the unknown print is compared with the suspected or questioned print by means of the ridge details (see Figure 7). Twelve ridge details or "points" is acceptable in court to "prove" that two prints were made by the same person. When evidence is introduced in this manner it is referred to as "associative physical evidence". Any twelve ridge details will provide a match even if all twelve points are the more common ridge endings. Courts will generally accept less than twelve points for identification purposes when the comparable ridge details are more unique (i.e., islands, bifurcations, bridges, etc.).

VII. Fingerprint Classification

Fingerprint classification allows for a systematic placement of fingerprints into categories so that they can be easily located in files. A classification formula, consisting of numbers and letters written above and below a horizontal line, is utilized with all ten fingers. There are six classification divisions: Key, Major, Primary, Secondary, Sub-Secondary, and Final. The Key and Major Division are sub-classifications which are used when fingerprint collection files are extensive. The Primary, Secondary, Sub-Secondary, and Final are fingerprint classification divisions developed by Sir Edward R. Henry and, subsequently, known as the Henry system (5).

34

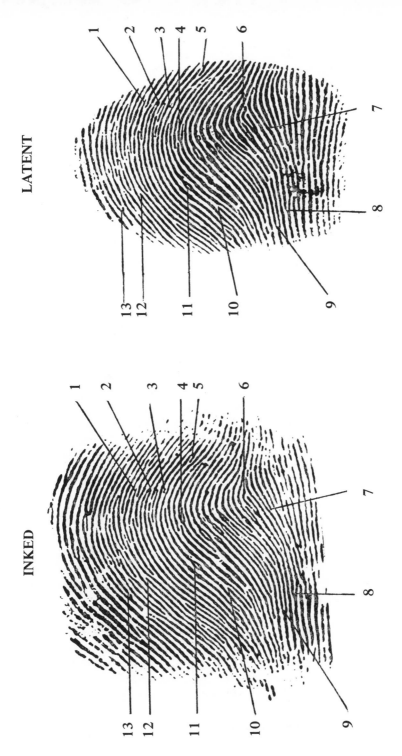

LATENT

INKED

FIGURE 7. FINGERPRINT COMPARISON.

35

The first step in the classification process is to mark the pattern symbol below each fingerprint pattern known as blocking out (see Figure 8). The following symbols are used:

1. Arch - A or a

2. Tented Arch - T or t

3. Radial Loop - R or r

4. Ulnar Loop - /(left hand), \(right hand)

5. Whorl - W or w

Capital letters are used for the index finger (unless that finger is an ulnar loop). Lower case letters are used for all other fingers (unless the finger is a ulnar loop).

Fingerprint classification uses ridge counting to a large extent. Ridge counting is a method of counting the number of ridges in a fingerprint pattern on a imaginary straight line drawn from the point of the delta to the point of the core. The method of ridge counting is different for loops and whorls (see Figure 9).

In loops, the core and the delta are not counted. A "white space" must come between the first ridge and the delta which defines the first ridge. If the imaginary line bisects a bifurcation or an island, two ridges are counted. Dots and short ridges are counted if the imaginary line bisects them.

In whorls, three symbols are used to distinguish between the three types of whorls. I for Inner, M for Meeting, and O for Outer are placed in the upper right hand corner of a whorl print. The selection of whorl types is determined by this sequence:

RIGHT HAND

1. Thumb	2. Index	3. Middle	4. Ring	5. Little
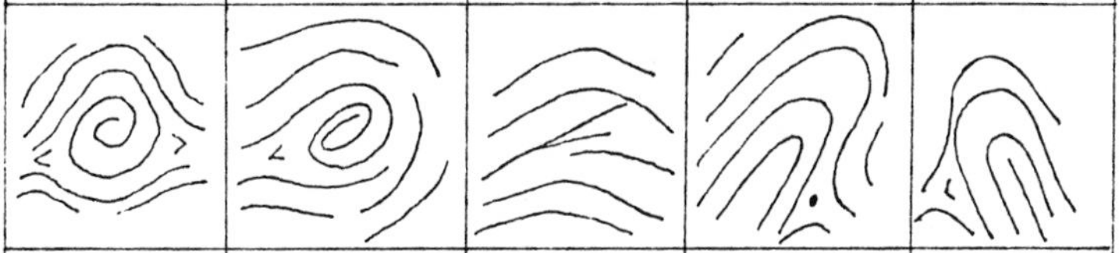				
w	W	a	r	\

LEFT HAND

6. Thumb	7. Index	8. Middle	9. Ring	10. Little
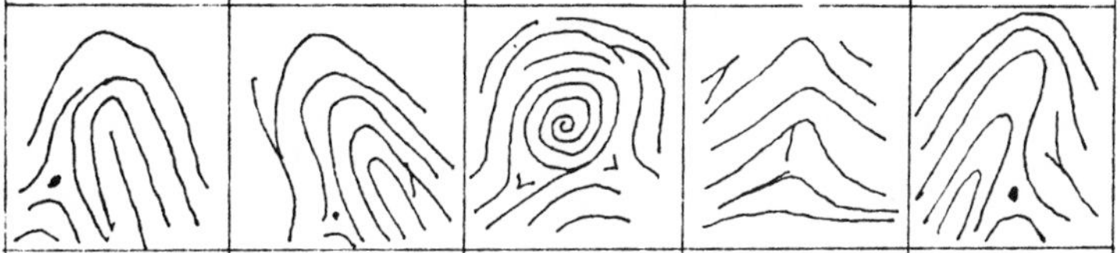				
r	R	w	t	/

FIGURE 8. BLOCKING OUT.

37

LOOP

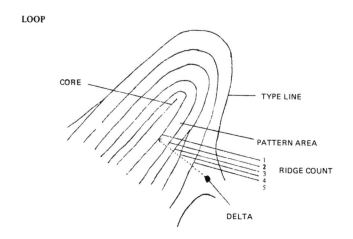

CORE

TYPE LINE

PATTERN AREA

RIDGE COUNT

1
2
3
4
5

DELTA

WHORL

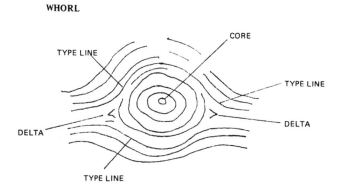

CORE

TYPE LINE

TYPE LINE

DELTA

DELTA

TYPE LINE

FIGURE 9.   LOOPS AND WHORLS.

1. Locate the deltas.

2. Establish a tracing line by beginning with a ridge at the lower point of the extreme left delta and continuing to the point nearest (opposite) the extreme right delta.

3. Count the number of ridges between the tracing line and the right delta.

4. If the traced ridge passes inside or above the right delta with three or more ridges coming between the traced line and the delta, the whorl is typed as Inner and indicated by the letter I.

5. If the traced ridge passes outside or below the right delta and there are three or more ridges coming between the traced line and the delta, the whorl is typed as Outer and indicated by the letter O.

6. If the traced ridge meets the right delta or there are two or less ridges coming between the traced line and the delta, the whorl is typed as Meeting and indicated by the letter M.

7. When tracing a ridge and the ridge forks, continue the trace on the lower branch of the fork. If the tracing ridge ends before the delta, continue the trace on the next lower ridge (see Figure 10).

Primary Classification

The primary classification consists of assigning fixed numerical values to each of the ten fingers. These fixed values are designated in pairs. The values are used for whorls only; no value is assigned to loops or arches. Beginning with the right thumb and using every odd number finger of both hands, the fixed numerical value in the corresponding box is added when a whorl

39

RIDGE TRACING

 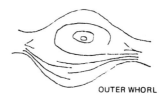

INNER WHORL OUTER WHORL

MEETING WHORL MEETING WHORL

FIGURE 10. WHORL TYPES.

appears. This sum, plus one, is the denominator for the primary classification fraction symbol. The numerator for the primary classification fraction symbol is found by beginning with the right index finger and using even numbered fingers. When a whorl appears in a corresponding box, the numbers are added plus one. Therefore, the lowest primary classification is 1/1 and the highest is 32/32.

Secondary Classification

The secondary classification involves the assignment of letters to the fingers. These symbols are also in the form of a fraction. The right hand symbols make up the numerator and the left hand symbols are the denominator. The index finger is always assigned a capital letter and the other fingers lower case letters:

1. Arch = A,a

2. Tented Arch = T,t

3. Radial Loop = R,r

4. Ulnar Loop = U,u

5. Whorl = W,w

For instance, if the right index finger were a whorl and the left index finger were a Ulnar loop = W/U.

Ulnar loops and whorls appearing on thumbs are ignored in secondary classification. If an ulnar loop or a whorl appears on the middle or ring finger and there is an arch, tented arch, or radial loop to their right, they are represented by a dash. If successive fingers have the same pattern type, a numerical value is placed with the letter. For instance, if a radial loop appears on the right middle and right ring finger, the classification would represent 2r.

41

Sub-Secondary Classification

In the sub-secondary classification, the thumbs and little fingers are not considered. The right hand fingers represent the numerator and the left hand fingers represent the denominator in a fraction symbol. For whorls, the symbols I (Inner), M (Meeting), and O (Outer) are used as determined by the procedure described earlier. Arches are not considered in sub-secondary classification. Loops are represented by I and O and based on the ridge count. A ridge count of one to nine for loops on index fingers is represented by the symbol I. A ridge count of one to ten for loops on middle fingers is represented by the symbol I. A ridge count greater than ten on middle fingers is assigned O. A ridge count of one to thirteen for loops on ring fingers is assigned I. A ridge count greater than thirteen is represented by O.

Final Classification

The final classification consists of assigning a ridge count number to the little fingers. Again, a fraction symbol is utilized using the right little finger as the numerator and left little finger as the denominator. If a loop appears on the right little finger, the ridges are counted and the number placed in the numerator with the sub-secondary classification fraction symbol. The complete final classification is that number. If no loop appears on the right little finger but does appear on the left, then the left little finger is utilized and the number placed in the denominator of the sub-secondary classification. If no loops appear on the little fingers, no final classification is used.

The Key

The key is placed to the left of the numerator, regardless of the finger on which it is found (right or left). The key is a ridge count of the first loop found in a set of ten fingerprints beginning with the right thumb. The little fingers are omitted.

Major Division

The major division considers only the thumbs. The symbols for the major division is written immediately to the right of the key in the numerator and on the extreme left in the denominator. If both the right and left thumbs are whorls, the symbols I, M, and O are utilized. If both thumbs are loops, the symbols S (small), M (medium), and L (large) are utilized in the major division fraction formula. Ridge counts are considered small (S) from one to eleven; medium (M) from twelve to sixteen; and, large (L) if the ridge count is seventeen or more. The right thumb is considered the numerator and the left thumb the denominator. If one thumb is a whorl and the other thumb is a loop, a combination of symbols is used respectively.

Figure 11 gives an example of a classification of ten fingerprints. Figure 12 depicts a chart for the fingerprint classification procedure.

RIGHT HAND

1. Thumb (16)	2. Index (16)	3. Middle (8)	4. Ring (8)	5. Little (4)
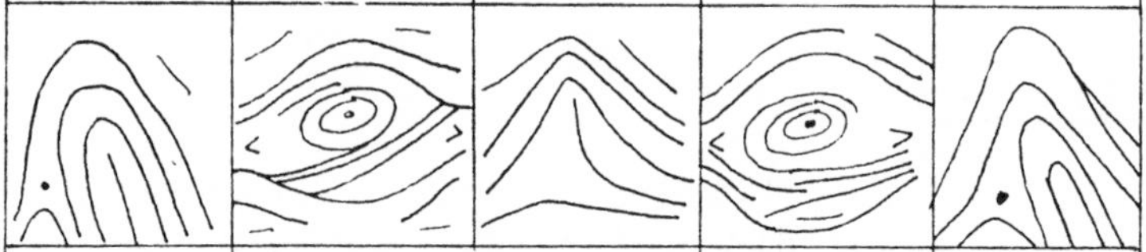				
u	W	t	w	u

LEFT HAND

6. Thumb (4)	7. Index (2)	8. Middle (2)	9. Ring(1)	10. Little (1)

a	W	u	u	w

PRIMARY CLASSIFICATION:
Numerator = 16 + 8 + 1 (even) + 1 = 26
Denominator = 2 (odd, box 7) + 1 = 3
Primary Classification = $\frac{26}{3}$

SECONDARY CLASSIFICATION: $\frac{Wtwu}{aW2uw}$

SUB – SECONDARY CLASSIFICATION: $\frac{IO}{MII}$

FINAL: 2

KEY: 2

MAJOR DIVISION: $\frac{S}{a}$

FINGERPRINT CLASSIFICATION:

Key	Major	Primary	Secondary	Sub--Secondary	Final
2	S	26	Wtwu	IO	2
	a	3	aW2uw	MII	

FIGURE 11. CLASSIFICATION.

KEY	MAJOR	PRIMARY	SECONDARY	SUB SECONDARY	FINAL
Example: 11	S	26	aW2t	IIO	6
	I	3	W	IMO	
RIDGE COUNT	RT. THUMB	EVEN WHORLS	RT. HAND	RT. HAND	RT. LITTLE
	LEFT THUMB	ODD WHORLS	LEFT HAND	LEFT HAND	
Ridge Count of First Loop. Omit Little Fingers. Use a Number. Always place the Number in the Numerator.	Ridge Count of Thumb. Use a Symbol. Right= = Numerator. Left = Denominator.	Values of Whorls in Fingerprint Boxes (even and odd) plus 1. Use a Number. Evens = Numerator. Odds = Denominator.	Use Symbols for all Fingers. Use Capital Letter for Index on both Hands. Right = Numerator. Left = Denominator.	Ridge Count of 3 Middle Fingers. Omit Arches. Use Symbols. Right = Numerator. Left = Denominator.	Ridge Count of Loops on Right Little Finger. No Loop on Right Little use Left Little and place the number in the Denominator. No Loops on either finger - Omit.

FIGURE 12.   FINGERPRINT CLASSIFICATION PROCEDURE CHART.

References

1. Cummins, Harold and Midlo, Charles, _Finger Prints, Palms, and Soles: An Introduction to Dermatoglyphics,_ (New York: Dover Publications, Inc., 1961).

2. Jantz, R.L., "Sex and Race Differences in Finger Ridge-Count Correlations," _American Journal of Physical Anthropology,_ 46:171-176, 1977.

3. Dalrymple, B.E., Duff, J.M., and Menzel, E.R. "Inherent Fingerprint Luminescence - Detection by Laser," _J. of Forensic Sciences,_ 22, No. 1 (1977), 106-115.

4. Mislove, J. (Ed.) _Dura-Print Investigators' Report,_ 1, No. 3 (1983).

5. Henry, Edward R., _Classification and Uses of Finger Prints,_ 8th Edition, (London: H.M. Stationery Office, 1937).

Additional Reading

Allison, Harrison C., _Personal Identification,_ (Boston: Holbrook Press, 1973).

Bridges, B.C., _Practical Fingerprinting,_ (New York: Funk and Wagnalls, 1963).

Brooks, A.J., Jr., "Techniques for Finding Latent Prints," _Fingerprint and Identification Magazine,_ 5:113, 1972.

Crown, W.A., "The Development of Latent Finger Prints with Ninhydrin," _Journal of Criminal Law, Criminology, and Police Science,_ 258, 1969.

Cummins, Harold, and Midlo, Charles, Finger Prints, Palms and Soles, (New York: Dover Publications, 1961).

DeAngelis, Francis J., Criminalistics for the Investigator, (Encino, California: Glencoe Publishing Co., Inc., 1980).

Federal Bureau of Investigation, The Science of Fingerprints, (Washington, D.C.: Government Printing Office).

Miller, L.S., Brown, A.M., and Carimi, N.J. Criminal Evidence Laboratory Manual: An Introduction to the Crime Laboratory, (Johnson City, TN: Institute of Social Sciences and Arts, Inc., 1985).

Morris, H.R., et al., "Some of the New Developments in the Chemical Detection of Latent Fingerprints," Police Research Bulletin, 21:31, 1973.

Osterburg, James W., The Crime Laboratory, 2d Edition, (New York: Clark Boardman Co., Ltd., 1982).

Thomas, G.L., "The Physics of Fingerprints," Criminologist, 30:21,1973.

3

SEROLOGY

Serology denotes the study of physiological fluids of the body (i.e., blood, semen, urine, tears, perspiration, saliva, and lymph). Body fluids are important in the human identification process. In most cases, a fresh and sufficient quantity of body fluids can be matched to an individual. Sex offenses, paternity disputes, and body fluid evidence at a crime scene are all important in forensic serological identification.

I. Blood

Blood is composed of a complex mixture of cells, enzymes, proteins, and inorganic substances. The liquid portion of blood is called plasma. Plasma carries solid substances consisting mainly of red and white blood cells and platelets (an aid for clotting). On the surface of red blood cells are millions of chemical structures called antigens. It is antigens that give red blood cells their typing characteristics.

Blood cannot be used as a positive source of human identification, but it is very useful in the elimination process. One can demonstrate that a sample of blood is not that of another individual if his blood type differs from the sample. If there is a match of blood type, the laws of probability come into play and the evidence becomes circumstantial.

Blood Typing

Human blood can be typed in more than fifteen antigen typing systems. Of these, the ABO, MN, and Rh systems are the most important and most recognized for forensic identification purposes.

The ABO system is categorized into four types: A (42% of the human population), B (10% of the human population), O (45% of the human population), and AB (3% of the human population). If an individual is type A, this indicates that each red blood cell has A antigens located on its surface. Type B individuals have B antigens on the surface of each red blood cell. AB individuals have both A and B antigens on the surfaces of red blood cells. Type O individuals have neither A nor B antigens. Therefore, it is the presence or absence of the A and B antigens on the red blood cells that determines an individual's blood type in the ABO system.

Another human blood factor commonly used for human identification is the Rh factor. Rh stands for Rhesus, a monkey species that was first used in the discovery of the Rh factor. The Rh factor is a blood antigen that is also called D antigen. Individuals having the D antigen on red blood cells are Rh positive and those not having the D antigen are Rh negative. In addition to positive and negative, the Rh factor can be further divided into at least 36 genotypes.

The fundamental principle of blood typing is that for every antigen there is a specific antibody. Each antibody symbol contains the prefix "anti" followed by the name of the antigen for which it is specific. Therefore, anti-A is specific only for A antigen, anti-B for B antigen, and anti-D for D antigen (Rh factor). The serum containing the antibody is referred to as an anti-serum. Anti-H antibody is a lectin (produced from vegetable protein) which is specific for type O red blood cells. For example, if an anti-serum containing anti-A is added to red blood cells carrying the antigen A, the two will immediately combine, causing the antibody to attach itself to the cells. The attachment or clumping together is known as agglutination (see Figures 13 and 14).

The MN system is also useful in human identification, particularly when one is dealing

50

ANTI - A SERUM ADDED TO WHOLE HUMAN BLOOD	ANTI - B SERUM ADDED TO WHOLE HUMAN BLOOD	ANTIGEN PRESENT	BLOOD TYPE
AGGLUTINATION	NO AGGLUTINATION	A	A
NO AGGLUTINATION	AGGLUTINATION	B	B
AGGLUTINATION	AGGLUTINATION	A and B	AB
NO AGGLUTINATION	NO AGGLUTINATION	Neither A Nor B	O

FIGURE 13. BLOOD TYPING WITH KNOWN ANTISERUM.

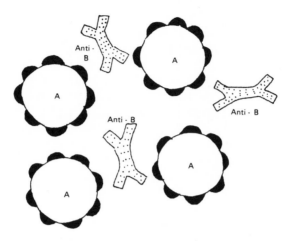

RED BLOOD CELLS WITH A ANTIGEN WILL NOT AGGLUTINATE WITH B ANTIBODIES

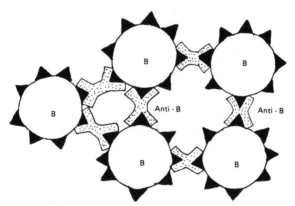

RED BLOOD CELLS WITH B ANTIGEN WILL AGGLUTINATE WITH B ANTIBODIES

FIGURE 14.   AGGLUTINATION PROCESS.

with dried blood stains. The MN system can be categorized into three separate populations: 1) Group M (approximately 28% of the human population); 2) Group N (approximately 22% of the human population); and, 3) Group MN (approximately 50% of the human population). In addition to the MN antigens, another factor has occasionally been included known as the S antigen factor. The S type is found present (indicated by a capital S) or absent (indicated with the lower case s) with an M, N, or MN type.

Enzymes contained in human blood are also used for forensic identification purposes. Enzymes are proteins that have important functions in regulating many of the body's chemical reactions.

Of particular importance to human identification is the ability to test human blood for social distinction. Several distinctive blood antigens and enzymes are found more frequently (or entirely) in the negroid race than in other races of man. By finding such antigens and enzymes in a human blood sample, one could conclude negroid race with a better than 90 percent accuracy (1).

Blood Stains

A criminal investigator will frequently find dried blood stains at the scene of a crime rather than fresh liquid blood. In some cases dried blood stains are difficult to locate, particularly on dark colored fabrics. The use of ultraviolet or infrared illumination may help locate such "invisible" blood stains. Blood stains appear as opaque patches under ultraviolet and infrared illumination.

In some cases it is necessary to make a preliminary screening of suspected blood stains in order to establish the fact that the stain is actually blood. A number of tests are available which, if positive, indicate a stain as blood.

However, a positive reaction of any preliminary screening test does not prove the presence of human blood. Such tests must be followed up with specific laboratory tests before conclusions are made. There are six common preliminary screening tests for blood available to field investigators:

1. <u>Benzidine Test.</u> The preparation of the reagent involves mixing 0.3 grams of benzidine with 100 ml of ethanol and 0.3 ml of glacial acetic acid. A positive reaction occurs if a blue color appears on the suspected blood stain after adding a few drops of the benzidine reagent, followed by a few drops of hydrogen peroxide.

2. <u>Orthotolidine Test.</u> The reagent is prepared by mixing 1.6 grams of O-tolidine with 40 ml of ethanol, 30 ml of glacial acetic acid, and 30 ml of distilled water. A few drops of the reagent is added to the suspected bloodstain, followed by a few drops of hydrogen peroxide. If positive, a green or blue color appears on the stain.

3. <u>Leuco-Malachite Test.</u> The reagent is prepared by mixing 3.2 grams of sodium perborate with 0.1 gram of leuco-malachite green, 66 ml of glacial acetic acid, and 33 ml of distilled water. Hydrogen peroxide is used with the reagent in the same manner as the other tests above. A positive reaction is reflected by the development of a bright green color on the suspected blood stain.

4. <u>Phenolphthalein Test.</u> A stock solution is prepared by mixing 2 grams of phenolphthalein with 20 grams of potassium hydroxide, and 100 ml of distilled water. This mixture is refluxed with 20 grams of powdered zinc for approximately two hours until the solution becomes colorless. The stock solution should be stored in a dark bottle with some zinc added to keep it in a reduced form and refrigerated. A working reagent is prepared

by mixing 20 ml of the stock solution with 80 ml of ethanol. A stain extract is produced from the suspected blood stain and placed on white filter paper. A few drops of the reagent is added to the filter paper followed by a few drops of hydrogen peroxide. If the stain is positive for blood, a pink color will develop on the filter paper. This test is also known as the Kastle-Meyer test (2: 650).

5.   Luminol Test. The reagent is prepared by mixing 0.1 gram of 3 - aminophthalhydrazide with 0.5 grams of sodium carbonate, 0.7 grams of sodium perborate, and 100 ml of distilled water. A suspected blood stain is sprayed with the luminol reagent and placed in a totally darkened room. If the stain is positive, blue-white luminous spots will appear on the stained area. This is a useful test when searching large areas for blood stains, such as carpeted rooms or walls.

6.   Tetramethylbenzidine Test. The preparation of the reagent involves mixing 2 grams of tetramethylbenzidine in 100 ml of glacial acetic acid. A few drops of the reagent is added to the suspected bloodstain followed by a few drops of hydrogen peroxide. A positive reaction is indicated by the development of a yellow-green color on the suspected blood stain.

None of the preliminary screening tests are completely specific for blood because they detect the presence of peroxidases which are found in several chemicals and in other biological fluids. The benzidine test was, for many years, recommended as the simpliest test and one which would not harm the blood stain itself. However, due to the carcinogenic nature of the benzidine test, it has been replaced by the tetramethylbenzidine test. The test is highly sensitive and, if found to be negative, there is little point in proceeding further with other tests.

Because preliminary screening tests are used for field purposes and test only for peroxidase activity, a specific test for hemoglobin must be conducted for conclusive proof that the stain is blood. The characteristic pigment contained in blood is hemoglobin and only if this is established as being present in a stain can it be said with certainty that the stain is blood. The crime laboratory may use one or more tests for hemoglobin. Two of the more common tests are the Hemoglobin Crystal Tests (Teichmann, Wagenaar, and Takayama Methods) and Spectroscopic Examination (3). The crystal tests are based upon the formation of hemoglobin derivative crystals such a hematin, hemin, and hemochromogen.

HEMATIN (TEICHMANN) TEST - Preparation
and Procedure:

> Potassium chloride 0.1g
> Potassium bromide 0.1g
> Potassium iodide 0.1g
> Glacial acetic acid 100 ml

1. Place a small amount of the questioned blood material on a microscopic slide. Add a cover slip.

2. Let a drop of the reagent flow under the cover slip and touch the dried crust. Avoid air bubbles.

3. With a small flame, gently heat the slide until bubbles form under the cover slip.

4. Examine the slide under a microscope to determine if hematin crystals have formed. The crystals are rhombic or prismatic in shape, dark brown in color, and approximately 10 microns in length. Crystal formation confirms the stain is blood.

ACETONE - CHLOR-HEMIN (WAGENAAR) TEST -
Preparation and Procedure:

>   Acetone
>   HCL (10% v/v)

A few drops of acetone are added to the bloodstain
followed by a drop of diluted hydrochloric acid
(HCL). Crystals form at room temperature if the
stain is blood.

TAKAYAMA (HEMOCHROMOGEN) TEST - Preparation and
Procedure:

>   Sodium hydroxide (10%v/v) 5 ml
>   Pyridine 5 ml
>   Glucose (100g/100ml) 5 ml
>   Glass Distilled Water 16 ml

1.   Place a small portion of the suspected
     bloodstain on a microscopic slide and add a
     cover slip.

2.   Let two drops of the Takayama reagent flow
     under the cover slip.

3.   Heat the slide with a low flame.

4.   Two forms of pink colored crystals will form
     in a few minutes and are observable under a
     microscope if positive for blood.

Spectroscopic examination is based upon the
identification of hemoglobin and its derivatives
through their specific absorption spectra.

Once conclusive proof has been established
that the stain is blood, the next step is the
determination of the species of origin - is it
human blood?

Tests to determine human blood generally
utilize an antisera which tests for specific
proteins found in human blood. In this manner,

tests can be performed to determine the origin of species of a blood stain (i.e., man, rabbit, cow, deer, etc.). There are several such tests available for use in the crime laboratory. Such tests include:

1. The Ring Test

2. Antihuman Globulin Consumption Test

3. Precipitation Reaction (Gel Diffusion) Test

4. Mixed Antiglobulin Test

5. Passive Haemagglutination Method

6. Gel Electrophoresis

7. Latex Particle Agglutination Test

The standard tests for human blood are the precipitin reaction tests. Precipitin tests are based on the fact that when animals (usually rabbits) are injected with human blood, antibodies are formed that react with the human blood to neutralize its' presence. These antibodies can be recovered from the animal and isolated in a blood serum known as human antiserum. Similarly, by injecting rabbits with the blood of other known animals, almost any kind of animal antiserum can be produced. Many game wardens use animal antiserum to test for deer and other animal blood in the possession of poachers to use as evidence for illegal hunting.

A number of tests (listed above) have been devised for performing precipitin tests on bloodstains. The standard method is to place an extract of the questioned bloodstain (or any protein of human origin) on top of human antiserum in a test tube. Human blood and proteins will react specifically with antibodies present in the antiserum. This reaction is indicated by the formation of a cloudy ring (precipitation) between

58

the questioned bloodstain extract and the antiserum (the Ring Test, see Figure 15).

Another precipitin test, known as Gel Diffusion (Figure 15), takes advantage of the fact that antibodies and antigens will move forward toward each other (diffuse) in an agar gel-coated plate. The bloodstain extract and human antiserum are placed in separate holes in the gel plate. If the blood is human, a precipitation line will form where the antigens and antibodies meet. By the same token, antigens and antibodies can be induced to move toward each other under the influence of an electrical field (Gel Electrophoresis).

Precipitin tests are very sensitive and require only a small amount of blood for testing. Human bloodstains and tissue dried for over fifteen years have still been known to give positive reactions with precipitin tests.

Once it has been determined that the bloodstains are human, it may become necessary in most cases to type the blood in order to determine if the bloodstain could have come from a particular individual. There are certain difficulties attached to the identification of bloodstains which do not exist when liquid whole blood is tested. Red blood cells usually do not remain intact once the blood has dried to a stain. Antigens found in dried, segmented, and broken up red blood cells from a bloodstain are still capable of being grouped, however. The Absorption-Elution technique is one method of typing bloodstains. The procedure involves the use of both A and B antiserum placed on the bloodstain and allowing the antibodies to combine with their specific antigens. Those antibodies that do not combine are washed away from the bloodstain. The bloodstain is then heated which allows for the antibody-antigen bond to break free (elution). When the eluted antibodies are placed in known red blood cells, they will or will not agglutinate in the same manner as typing whole blood. In this manner, the ABO group can be

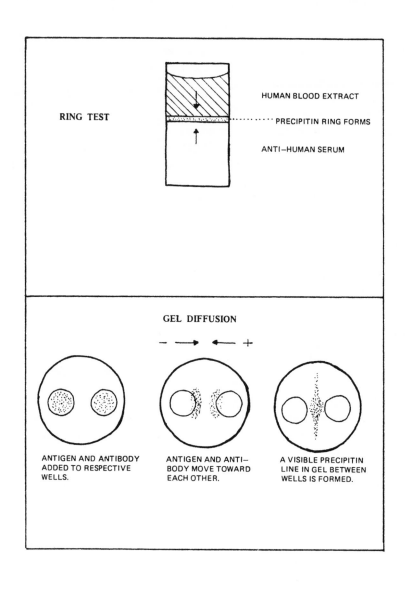

RING TEST

HUMAN BLOOD EXTRACT

PRECIPITIN RING FORMS

ANTI—HUMAN SERUM

GEL DIFFUSION

− → ← +

ANTIGEN AND ANTIBODY ADDED TO RESPECTIVE WELLS.

ANTIGEN AND ANTI—BODY MOVE TOWARD EACH OTHER.

A VISIBLE PRECIPITIN LINE IN GEL BETWEEN WELLS IS FORMED.

FIGURE 15.   PRECIPITIN REACTION TESTS.

identified. This technique is sensitive enough to type bloodstains on thread fibers one-half inch in length. Stains eleven years and older have been typed using the Absorption-Elution method (see Figure 16).

In addition to ABO testing of dried bloodstains, MN and Rh antigens have been successfully identified in dried bloodstains. At least five antigens in the Rh factor may be detected in dried bloodstains. These five factors are known as C, D, E, c, and e.

Certain enzymes can be found in whole and dried red blood cells that can be used for human identification purposes. The following enzymes can be satisfactorily detected in human bloodstains:

1. Phosphoglucomutase (PGM)

2. Adenylate Kenase (AK)

3. Adenosine Deaminase (ADA)

4. 6-Phosphogluconate Dehydrogenase (6-PGD)

5. Glucose-6-Phosphate Dehydrogenase (G-6-PD)

6. Erythrocyte Acid Phosphatase (EAP)

7. Glutamate-Pyruvate Transaminase (GPT)

8. Esterase D (EsD)

Some of these enzymes exist in different protein forms which increases the value of blood as an identification method. For instance, Phosphoglucomutase exists in three forms (PGM^1, PGM^2, and PGM^{2-1}) and Erythrocyte Acid Phosphatase exists in six forms (EAP^A, EAP^B, EAP^C, EAP^{CA}, and EAP^{CB}).

STEP 1

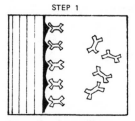

Blood stained material is treated
with antiserum. Antibody binds
to specific antigen.

STEP 2

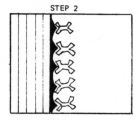

Excess antibodies are washed away.
Specific antibody remains bound
to antigen.

STEP 3

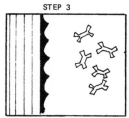

Antibodies are freed by elution
from antigens.

Known red blood cells are
added.

STEP 4

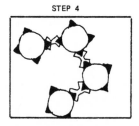

Agglutination occurs if antigens
present on the added red blood
cells are same as blood stain.

FIGURE 16.   ABSORPTION — ELUTION PROCESS.

Because antigens, enzymes, and proteins occur independently of each other, the probability of a dried bloodstain having a particular combination of these factors present can be determined. In this manner, a statistical probability of occurrence in a given population can narrow down a suspect and make for excellent circumstantial evidence.

Deterioration of Blood

Blood deteriorates or denatures rapidly, depending upon conditions, amounts, and environment. However, blood group antigens and other gene products in blood (i.e., enzymes) deteriorate at different rates. Usually, bloodstains which have had an opportunity to dry quickly retain their "freshness" for longer periods than those remaining wet or in moist environments. Freshness of dried blood may last only a few hours or days to many years. The antigens of the ABO system seem particularly able to withstand the passage of time. Enzymes in red blood cells may vary in deterioration or denaturing time ranging from one day to over a month depending upon environmental conditions.

Many criminal investigators feel they must submit questioned bloodstains found at a crime scene with known blood samples to a crime laboratory for comparison purposes. It is not uncommon for investigators to wait several weeks or months before submitting dried bloodstains to a laboratory for identification. Investigators should always submit blood or any biological evidence to a laboratory as soon as possible for identification. If and when known blood samples are acquired for comparison with questioned samples, they can be sent to a laboratory for identification and the crime lab reports may be used for comparison purposes.

Sexing of Bloodstains

There have been several attempts at determining the sex of the individual from blood and bloodstains. Although there have been some successes in determining sex from blood samples and stains, there is presently no reliable method (4). There are proven methods of determining menstrual blood which have been used in forensic cases, however (5).

Handling of Bloodstain Evidence

1. Do not put evidence in plastic bags, as a warm moist environment will promote deterioration.

2. Do not put more than one item of evidence in the same bag. A stain originally on one item may be transferred to another.

3. Do not put clothes with wet bloodstains into an evidence bag.

4. Do put evidence in paper bags; each individually labeled and sealed.

5. Do allow wet bloodstains on clothing to air dry under normal room temperature before packaging.

6. Do bring or mail evidence to a crime laboratory as soon as possible.

7. Liquid blood samples should be taken by medical personnel. Two 10cc tubes of blood, one with and one without preservative, should be submitted to a crime laboratory.

8. Store all liquid blood in a refrigerator; not frozen, until delivered to a crime laboratory.

II. Semen Stains

A normal healthy male will ejaculate approximately 2 to 5 milliliters (ml) of semen at coitus. Unless the male individual has had a vasectomy or is sterile, the normal sperm count will range between 70,000,000 and 150,000,000 sperm cells (spermatozoa) per milliliter of semen (sperm comprises roughly 10 percent of the total ejaculate). A sperm count of less than 50,000,000 per ml is indicative of male infertility. Spermatozoa generally measure one five thousandth of an inch long (1/5000 inch). A sperm cell (spermatozoon) normally survives in the vagina of a living woman for only 30 minutes to 6 hours. Motility for several days is still possible in ideal conditions. Nonmotile sperm may be found for periods up to 14 hours or even longer in rare cases. Within a day or so, sperm are totally dissolved or excreted by the living female.

Attempts have been made to fix the time of intercourse by the death rate of sperm. However, the length of time a spermatozoon can survive after ejaculation varies so greatly with differences in environmental temperature, body temperature, physical health of the female and male, use of contraceptives and spermatocides that it is of little use as a means of establishing the time for intercourse. Semen ejaculate is an alkali (the reason for the faint ammonia odor). Vaginal secretions are acidic (properties opposed to those of alkalis). Since vaginal secretions are hostile to sperm cells, a spermatoozoon is unlikely to survive longer than 6 hours in normal circumstances. However, for forensic purposes, it would be difficult to determine "normality" for time estimation of intercourse.

Seminal stains are identified by similar methods as bloodstains. Seminal stains have a white glistening appearance on dark material. The stains will stiffen fabric after drying. They also fluorescence (glow) under ultraviolet illumination.

The most common test for semen is the Acid Phosphatase Test (6). This test identifies the presence of the enzyme acid phosphatase in seminal stains. Human seminal fluid will contain 20 to 400 times as much acid phosphatase as other human fluids. Semen stains also produce characteristic crystal formations with an iodine reagent solution known as the Florence Test (7). The Florence Test is used to test for the content of choline which is also found in high concentrations in semen.

The acid phosphatase test is available commercially and is somewhat difficult and expensive to prepare. The Florence test, however, is prepared by adding 1.7g of potassium iodide and 2.5g of iodine crystals to 30ml of distilled water. A portion of the suspected stain is dried on a microscopic slide and a cover slip is added. A drop or two of the Florence reagent is allowed to flow under the cover slip and observed under a microscope at 100x. If brown colored rhombic crystals are formed, the stain contains a high concentration of choline and is characteristic of the presence of semen. The formation of the brown crystals are a result of choline reacting with the iodine/iodide complex to form periodide of choline.

The fact that acid phosphatase and choline is found in other biological fluids indicates that the test is not absolute proof of semen. The absolute proof is the finding of spermatozoa in the stain or serum.

III. Vaginal Stains

Vaginal stains have a number of characteristics in common with seminal fluid (apart from the presence of sperm). Anti-human semen serum will cross-react with vaginal fluid in the same manner as blood tests. There are proven methods of distinguishing between the phosphates of seminal and vaginal secretions. Such tests are particularly useful in rape cases involving men who have had vasectomies or are sterile.

IV. Secretors

Blood group substances found in other body fluids are presently confined to the ABO system. Not all individuals secrete their corresponding blood groups in their body fluids, however. About 75 percent of the human population are known as secretors. Secretors usually produce ABO blood group substances in high concentrations in seminal fluid, saliva, vaginal secretion, and gastric juices. In other body fluids (i.e., sweat, tears, urine) the concentration is fairly low.

Even in non-secretors, there are trace amounts of substances that can be detected. For instance, saliva stains are identifiable through the enzyme Amylase (an enzyme that converts starch into sugars). Urine stains may be identified by ultraviolet illumination. Urine will fluorescene with a yellowish color. Urine may also be heated which will produce the characteristic odor.

Mixture of Stains

Stain and fluid mixing is a common occurrence in rape and assault cases. Blood and saliva samples are usually available from the victim of such crimes and such samples can be tested for the presence or absence of other groups or types of body fluids. Any substance that appears in a stain or fluid that is absent from the victim's sample is proof of a mixture.

V. Collecting Body Fluids And Stains For Lab Examination

In collecting samples of body fluids or fluid stains for crime laboratory examination, it is important that a control for variables be exercised by the investigator. There is a tendency for criminal investigators to be overly optimistic regarding the ability of crime laboratory technicians in performing scientific analyses. It is important that the crime laboratory receive, as much as possible, those samples and items for comparison that are available. For instance, bloodstains on a shirt should not be cut out by the investigator and submitted to a laboratory. Instead, the entire shirt should be submitted. The purpose of this procedure is to determine if there is anything present on the fabric that may contribute to, or interfere with, the scientific examination of the stain. Perspiration, detergents, or deodorants on the shirt may yield misleading results concerning grouping tests.

In addition, the sufficiency of samples should also be considered. Although it is not possible to control the amount of questioned fluid or stain material, it is usually possible to obtain sufficient quantities of test (known) samples of fluid. For instance, at least 5cc to 10cc of liquid blood should be taken from an individual for comparison with unknown or questioned stain material.

VI. Detecting Alcohol And Drugs In Serological Samples

Detecting alcohol and/or drugs in serological samples generally involve two processes of collection and analysis: 1) detection of alcohol/drugs in the blood or urine of living persons and 2) detection of alcohol/drugs or toxic substances in blood/urine or gastric juices of deceased persons. The actual laboratory analysis for detecting such foreign substances in serological samples is the same for living or deceased individuals.

Detection of alcohol in blood or urine samples usually involves one of two processes: 1) diffusion-desiccation (exposing the specimen to an oxidizing agent in a sealed container); or 2) distillation (heating the specimen to reflux or boil off the alcohol to be recovered). The distillation process is the more common of the two methods.

In detecting narcotics in serological samples, urine has been used with the most success. There are several urine tests available for various forms of narcotics. The use of these tests is referred to as a "drug screen". The chemical tests are time consuming and expensive. Most laboratories utilize chromotography or spectrophotometric instrumental analysis. These instrumental tests are also utilized for the detection of toxic chemicals in serological samples (e.g., arsenic, mercury, cyanide, carbon monoxide, etc.).

The collection of serological samples from individuals should be performed by medical personnel. The medical examiner should collect blood, urine, and gastric juices (e.g., bile) during autopsy for pathological examination when dealing with deceased individuals. The investigator should never assume that such examinations for the detection of alcohol/drugs/toxic substances are routinely made. The investigator must request that medical personnel perform such examinations to ascertain that the chain of evidence remains intact and ensure that the tests are performed.

References

1. Camps, Francis E., Gradwohl's Legal Medicine, 3rd Edition, (Chicago: Year Book Medical Publications, Inc., 1976), p. 150.

2. Glaister, J., "The Kastle-Meyer Test for the Detection of Blood," British Medical Journal, 1:650, 1926.

3. Lee, Henry C., "Identification and Grouping of Bloodstains," in Saferstein, Richard (Ed.), Forensic Science Handbook, (Englewood Cliffs, New Jersey: Prentice-Hall, Inc., 1982), pp. 278-279.

4. Camps, Gradwhol's Legal Medicine, 1 p. 150.

5. Camps, Gradwhol's Legal Medicine, 1 p. 150.

6. Kind, S.S., "The Acid Phosphatase Test," in Curry, A.S. (Ed.), Methods of Forensic Science, (New York: John Wiley and Sons, 1964).

7. Saferstein, Richard, Criminalistics: An Introduction to Forensic Science, 2nd Edition, (Englewood Cliffs, New Jersey: Prentice-Hall, Inc., 1981), p. 309.

Additional Reading

Baird, J.B., "The Individuality of Blood and Bloodstains," Journal of Canadian Society of Forensic Science , 11:83, 1978.

Camps, Francis E. (Ed.), Gradwohl's Legal Medicine, 3rd Edition, (Chicago: Year Book Medical Publications, Inc., 1976).

Culliford, B.J., The Examination and Typing of Bloodstains in the Crime Laboratory, (Washington, D.C.: Government Printing Office, 1971).

Culliford, B.J. and Nickolls, L.C., "The Benzidine Test: A Critical Review," Journal of Forensic Science, 9:175, 1964.

DeAngelis, Francis J., Criminalistics for the Investigator, (Encino, California: Glencoe Publishing Co., Inc., 1980).

Race, R.R. and Sanger, R., Blood Groups in Man, 6th Edition, (Oxford: Blackwell Scientific Publishers, 1975).

Saferstein, Richard, Criminalistics: An Introduction to Forensic Science, 2d Edition, (Englewood Cliffs, New Jersey: Prentice-Hall, Inc., 1981).

Saferstein, Richard (Ed.), Forensic Science Handbook, (Englewood Cliffs, New Jersey: Prentice-Hall, Inc. 1982).

Snyder, L.H., Blood Groups, (Minneapolis: Burgess Publishing Co., 1973).

Willott, G.M., "The Role of the Forensic Biologist in Cases of Sexual Assualt," Journal of the Forensic Science Society, 15:269, 1975.

4

HUMAN HAIR IDENTIFICATION

Identification of epidermal hair may be required in some criminal investigations. Human hair identification is particularly important in rape and assault cases where an exchange of hair may be made between the victim and the offender.

I. Hair Morphology

There are four types of hair that occur on the bodies of human beings: 1) Primordial; 2) Lanugo; 3) Vellus; and 4) Terminal. At approximately the third month of fetal life, primordial hair begins to grow on the lips, eyebrows, palms and soles of the feet. These primordial hairs are shed and replaced by lanugo hair. Lanugo hair are fine unpigmented hairs that cover the fetus up to approximately the sixth month. Vellus and some terminal hairs replace lanugo hair before birth. Vellus hair is spread uniformly over the body with the exception of the palms, soles, lips and nipples. Terminal hair replaces vellus at specific sites and at specific periods of life.

Human hair grows from an organ known as a hair follicle. The root of the hair grows from within the follicle. A mass of loose connective tissue known as the dermal papilla surrounds the root portion within the hair follicle.

Human hair is composed of keratins, proteins that interconnect to form stable fibrils. These keratin protein chains are complex due to multiple protein molecule cross-linking that produces the integral structure. This complex cross-linking makes hair extremely resistant to biological and chemical degradation.

The structure of human hair is made up of three major parts: 1) cuticle; 2) cortex; and, 3) medulla. The cuticle is composed of scales that surround the shaft of the hair. These scales are thin translucent layers of over-lapping cells that point upwards, away from the root. The cortex is composed of elongated, fusiform, keratinized filaments aligned in a regular array, parallel to the length of the hair. The material which surrounds these filaments is a cement-like amorphorous protein which contains amino acids and a high sulfur content. Air sacs called cortical fusi are interspersed among the keratinized cells of the cortex. The medulla is a canal-like structure of air sacs which gives strength and flexibility to the hair. The medulla usually appears darker than the cortex due to the presence of air sacs and color pigments (Figure 17).

The color of hair is due to melanin which is produced by special cells in the hair follicle called melanocytes. Melanin is found in pigment granules within the cortex of the hair. The shade of hair color is based on the amount, shape, and size of the pigment granules present in the cortex. Under the microscope, hair will show color as either black, brown or yellow. The only exception to this is true blond or true red hair which owes its color to a different substance known as phaeo-melanin. The aging process involves the gradual loss of melanin production which, in turn, produces no pigment granules and the result is white or gray hair.

The growth and replacement of human hair proceeds through three distinct phases: 1) Anagen; 2) Catagen; and 3) Telogen. Anagen phase is the phase of active growth. Cells in the dermal papilla of the follicle grow upwards to form the medulla, cortex, and cuticle scales. Hair grows in the anagen phase on an average of 1000 days. In the catagen phase, melanocytes in the follicle contract and cease to produce and distribute pigment granules. Keratinized cells continue to move up and differentiate into a hair

MORPHOLOGY

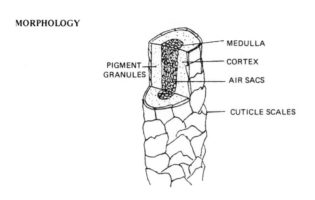

OVOID BODIES   PIGMENT GRANULES   CUTICLE SCALES

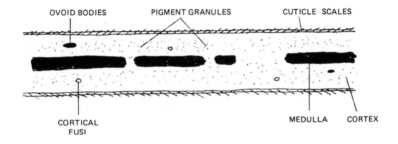

CORTICAL FUSI

MEDULLA   CORTEX

CROSS – SECTIONS (HUMAN)

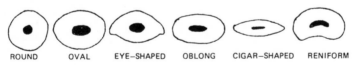

ROUND   OVAL   EYE–SHAPED   OBLONG   CIGAR–SHAPED   RENIFORM

FIGURE 17.   THE STRUCTURE OF HUMAN HAIR.

shaft consisting only of the cortex and inner root
sheath. The telogen phase is the resting stage of
growth. The hair is anchored in the follicle by a
club shaped root and is easily pulled from the
follicle. Germ cells within the hair follicle
begin the next generation of hair once the older
hair is pulled or falls away. On a healthy head,
one can expect to find 80%-90% of hair follicles
in the anagen phase, 2% in the catagen phase, and
10%-18% in the telogen phase. The telogen phase
rests for approximately 100 days (Figure 18).

II. Human Hair Identification

The first step in the identification of human
hair is the determination that the hair is,
indeed, human hair (Figure 19). The medullary
index is one method of determining human or animal
hair. The medullary index is found by dividing
the diameter of the medulla by the diameter of the
hair shaft then multiplying by one hundred
(medulla shaft x 100 = M.I.). If the result is
greater than 33%, the hair is non-human. Human
hair medulla diameters are seldom greater than one
third the diameter of the hair shaft. Cuticle
scales will be flat, small, and in irregular
patterns on human hair. Pigment granules in human
hair tend to have uniform distribution and are
translucent. Animal hair may have color pigment
"bands" and/or a concentration of pigment granules
around the medulla. If the root of the hair is
available, it will appear spear shaped if animal
and bulb shaped if human.

The second step is to determine the body
origin of the hair. There are at least twelve
areas on the human body that will produce hair
growth. These twelve areas are listed below with
the characteristics of each.

1. SCALP (HEAD): Usually from 25-125 microns in
                   diameter,   .40   millimeters
                   growth per day, small root,
                   tapered tip, little variation

76

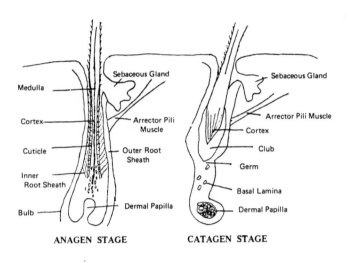

ANAGEN STAGE   CATAGEN STAGE

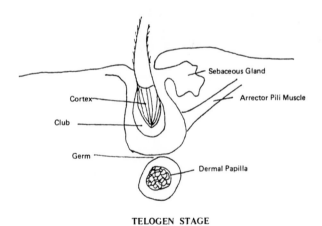

TELOGEN STAGE

FIGURE 18. STAGES OF HUMAN HAIR GROWTH.

77

CUTICLE SCALE PATTERNS

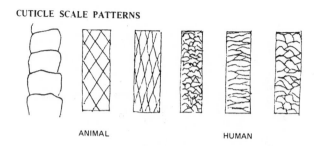

ANIMAL   HUMAN

MEDULLA PATTERNS

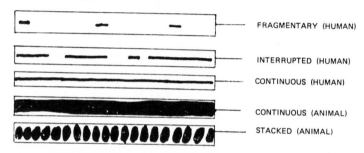

FRAGMENTARY (HUMAN)

INTERRUPTED (HUMAN)

CONTINUOUS (HUMAN)

CONTINUOUS (ANIMAL)

STACKED (ANIMAL)

ROOT

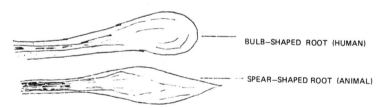

BULB—SHAPED ROOT (HUMAN)

SPEAR—SHAPED ROOT (ANIMAL)

FIGURE 19. HUMAN HAIR IDENTIFICATION.

from root (proximal end) to tip (distal end), medulla characteristics may be varied throughout the length of the shaft, cut tips are common occurrence, may be artificially treated (dyed or bleached).

2. PUBIC: Usually 10-60 millimeters long, coarse diameter with prominent diameter variations and "buckling," broad medulla, follicular "tags" common occurrence, cross-section appears twisted and constricted, may be straight, curved or spirally tufted.

3. VULVAR: Secondary pubic hair, finer and shorter than pubic hair, may have abraded characteristics.

4. CHEST: Pectoral, moderate to considerable diameter variation, usually has long-fine arched tips, usually longer than pubic hairs.

5. BEARD: Very coarse, usually 50-300 millimeters long, large root, irregular structure, often has a triangular shape by cross section, complex medullation, grows approximately .40 millimeters per day.

6. AXILLARY: Usually 10-15 millimeters long (armpit) (uncut), grows approximately .30 millimeters per day. Coarse, abraded or frayed

condition, usually straighter than pubic hair, contains many cortical fusi, sometimes has a yellowed and bleached appearance.

7. SUPER-CILIARY: (eyebrow)

Usually one centimeter in length, grows approximately .16 millimeters per day, curved, relatively coarse compared to length, has a smooth curved appearance, large medulla.

8. CILIARY: (eyelash)

Usually less than one centimeter in length, short, curved and pointed.

9. LIMB: (leg and arm)

Usually 3-6 millimeters in length, fine tips, irregular medullated, often indistinct or slight pigmentation.

10. EAR:

Fine downy hair.

11. BUTTOCKS:

Short, blunted tips, abraded.

12. NOSE:

Similar to beard hair, usually softer and slighter diameter than beard hair.

Racial origin may be determined by examining the diameter, cross-section, pigment granules, cuticle scales, and curliness (undulation) of the hair (Figure 20).

No two specimens of hair from a single person are identical in every detail. Variation is an integral part of the natural growth of hair. Any association between a known hair and a questioned hair should demonstrate that the unknown hair not only has the same traits as the known hair but the variations which occur in the unknown hair are similar to the variations in the known hair. For

80

RACE	DIAMETER	CROSS – SECTION	PIGMENT	CUTICLE	UNDULATION
NEGROID	60 - 90 um	Flat - Shaped	Dense and Clumped	Thin	Prevalent
CAUCASOID	70 - 100 um	Oval - Shaped	Evenly Distributed	Medium	Uncommon
MONGOLOID	90 - 120 um	Round - Shaped	Dense with Auburn color	Thick	Never

um = Microns (.001 mm or 1/25000 inch).

FIGURE 20.   RACIAL HAIR CHARACTERISTICS.

individuality, there must be sufficient unique characteristics in both the questioned and known hair to establish beyond doubt that both hairs came from the same person (1). Although this is a rare occurrence in forensic work, it is generally accepted that an association with the characteristics discussed here will provide sufficient evidence for an expert to determine that an unknown hair from a crime scene came from an individual suspect (2).

Two studies have attempted to establish statistical probabilities of finding the same human hair on other individuals. The Royal Canadian Mounted Police study found that if one human head hair found at a crime scene (questioned) is found to be similar to a representative hair from a suspect's head (known), the odds against the questioned hair originating from a different person are approximately 4500 to 1 (3). Gaudette's study revealed that the odds against two similar pubic hairs originating from two different individuals are approximately 800 to 1 (4). Because Negroid and Mongoloid hair exhibit less variation in characteristics than Caucasoid hair, it is expected that these odds would be somewhat less for individuals of the Negroid and Mongoloid races.

Known hair should be collected (combings) from the body of the suspect for comparison purposes. It should be remembered that hair can only be compared with hair from the same origin of the body due to the variation of hair morphology on a single individual. For instance, if pubic hair is found at the scene of a crime then pubic hair samples should be collected from the suspect for comparative purposes.

An example of a general hair identification and comparison form is depicted in Figure 21. A crime lab technician may use such a form to record his/her notes and findings when comparing known and questioned hairs. Such notes are invaluable for court testimony when referring to those

HUMAN HAIR EXAMINATION AND COMPARISON FORM

CASE NUMBER OR NAME: _____ DATE _____
EXAMINED BY _____
KNOWN HAIR OF: _____ SEX ___ RACE ___ AGE _____
KNOWN SAMPLES TAKEN BY: _____ DATE _____
QUESTIONED HAIR FOUND: _____
FOUND BY: _____ DATE _____

CHARACTERISTIC	KNOWN	QUESTIONED	SAME
I. TYPE 　1. Animal 　2. Human Vellus 　3. Human Terminal 　4. Other 　Notes:			
II. COLOR 　1. White 　2. Blonde 　3. Lt. Brown 　4. Brown 　5. Gray Brown 　6. Dk. Brown 　7. Gray 　8. Black 　9. Auburn 　10. Red 　Notes:			
III. BODY LOCATION 　1. Scalp 　2. Beard 　3. Nose 　4. Ear 　5. Eyebrow 　6. Eyelash 　7. Chest 　8. Axillary 　9. Limb 　10. Buttock 　11. Pubic 　12. Vulvar 　Notes:			

FIGURE 21a. HUMAN HAIR EXAMINATION AND COMPARISON FORM.

CHARACTERISTIC	KNOWN	QUESTIONED	SAME

IV. TIP CONDITION
  1. Partial
  2. Cut
  3. Split
  4. Crushed
  5. Frayed
  6. Natural Worn
 	
  Notes:			

V. LENGTH
  1. Under 1"
  2. 1 - 3"
  3. 3 - 5"
  4. 5 - 8"
  5. 8 - 12"
  6. 12 - 18"
  7. Over 18"
 	
  Notes:			

VI. DIAMETER OF SHAFT
  1. 20 - 40 um
  2. 40 - 60 um
  3. 60 - 80 um
  4. 80 - 100 um
  5. 100 - 120 um
 	
  Notes:			

VII. CONFIGURATION
  1. Undulating
  2. Kinky
  3. Wavy
  4. Straight
  5. Curved
  6. Other
 	
  Notes:			

VIII. ROOT
  1. Absent
  2. Bulbous
  3. Sheathed
  4. Tapered
  5. Other
 	
  Notes:			

FIGURE 21b. HUMAN HAIR EXAMINATION AND COMPARISON FORM.

HUMAN HAIR EXAMINATION AND COMPARISON FORM

CHARACTERISTIC	KNOWN	QUESTIONED	SAME

IX. CROSS SECTION
  1. Round
  2. Oval
  3. Eye-Shaped
  4. Oblong
  5. Cigar-Shaped
  6. Reniform
 	
Notes:			

X. PIGMENT DENSITY
  1. Absent
  2. Sparse
  3. Medium
  4. Heavy
 	
Notes:			

XI. PIGMENT SIZE
  1. Small Streaked
  2. Small Globs
  3. Medium Streaked
  4. Medium Globs
  5. Large Streaked
  6. Large Globs
 	
Notes:			

XII. PIGMENT DISTRIBUTION
  1. Uniform
  2. Peripheral
  3. Near Medulla
  4. Clusters
 	
Notes:			

XIII. MEDULLA
  1. Absent
  2. Continuous Opaque
  3. Continuous Translucent
  4. Continuous Opaque & Translucent
  5. Fragmentary Opaque
  6. Fragmentary Translucent
  7. Fragmentary Opaque & Translucent
 	
Notes:			

FIGURE 21c.   HUMAN HAIR EXAMINATION AND COMPARISON FORM.

HUMAN HAIR EXAMINATION AND COMPARISON FORM

CHARACTERISTIC	KNOWN	QUESTIONED	SAME

XIV. MEDULLARY INDEX
   1. Under 33%
   2. Over 33%
 	
  Notes:			

XV. CUTICLE SCALE SURFACE
   1. Smooth
   2. Slightly Serrated
   3. Gross Serration
 	
  Notes:			

XVI. SCALE PATTERN
   1. Imbricate
   2. Mosiac
   3. Regular Wave
   4. Irregular Wave
   5. Chevron
 	
  Notes:			

XVII. OVOID BODIES
   1. Present
   2. Absent
 	
  Notes:			

XVIII. CORTICAL FUSI
   1. Absent
   2. Abundant
   3. Few
 	
  Notes:			

XIX. COSMETIC TREATMENT
   1. Bleached
   2. Dyed
   3. Natural
   4. Teased
   5. Other
 	
  Notes:			

FIGURE 21d. HUMAN HAIR EXAMINATION AND COMPARISON FORM.

HUMAN HAIR EXAMINATION AND COMPARISON FORM

CASE NUMBER OR NAME: _____

DATE OF EXAMINATION: _____

PHOTOGRAPHIC RECORD:
1. None ___
2. Color Slides ___
3. Color Video-Tape ___

CONCLUSIONS

SIGNATURE OF EXAMINER: _____

HAIR EVIDENCE INFORMATION:
1. Label on Known Hair Samples: _____
2. Label on Questioned Hair Samples: _____
3. Are there other Known or Questioned Samples relating to this? Yes___ No___
   a. If Yes, state the Label information: _____
   b. If Yes, have these samples been mounted on slides?   Yes___ No ___
4. Where will the Hair Evidence be Located?
   a. Retained in Crime Lab?   Yes ___ No ___
   b. Returned to Requesting Agency?   Yes ___ No ___
   c. Name, Address, and Phone Number of Requesting Agency:

COURT INFORMATION:
1. Location of Court: _____
2. Date of Court: _____
3. Court Presentations: _____
4. Disposition of Case: _____

FIGURE 21e.   HUMAN HAIR EXAMINATION AND COMPARISON FORM.

characteristics that were similar or dissimilar in hair comparisons.

III. Typing Of Human Hair

Generally, hair does not contain the same serological material as body fluids and, therefore, cannot be "typed." The only exception is if the hair root still has connective tissues from the follicle or skin (indicative of forcible removal). The tissues adhering to the hair root may be typed as any other body tissue for secretors.

Several attempts have been made to individualize human hair, none of which have proved successful (4). ABO typing, scale pattern classification, neutron activation analysis (NAA), X-ray diffraction, and other methods have been researched with little success.

References

1. Bisbing, Richard E., "The Forensic Identification and Association of Human Hair," in Saferstein, Richard (Ed.), Forensic Science Handbook, (Englewood Cliffs, New Jersey: Prentice-Hall, Inc., 1982), p. 202.

2. Gaudette, B.D. and Keeping, E.S., "An Attempt at Determining Probabilities in Human Scalp Hair Comparison," Journal of Forensic Sciences, 19:599, 1974.

3. Gaudette, B.D., "Probabilities and Human Hair Comparisons," Journal of Forensic Sciences, 21:514, 1976.

4. Camps, Francis, E., Gradwohl's Legal Medicine, 3rd Edition, (Chicago: Year Book Medical Publications, Inc., 1976), p. 164.

Additional Reading

Basset, W.A.G., "Sex Determination by Sex Chromatin Identification in the Hair Root Sheath," Journal of Canadian Society of Forensic Science, 11:121, 1978.

Beeman, J., "The Scale Count of Human Hair," Journal of Criminal Law and Criminology, 32:572, 1942.

Bisbing, Richard E., "The Forensic Identification and Association of Human Hair," in Saferstein, Richard (Ed.), Forensic Science Handbook, (Englewood Cliffs, New Jersey: Prentice-Hall, Inc., 1982).

Garn, S.M., "Cross Sections of Undistorted Human Hair," Science, 105:238, 1947.

Gaudette, B.D., "Probabilities and Human Pubic Hair Comparisons," Journal of Forensic Science, 21:514, 1976.

Hicks, J.W., Microscopy of Hairs, (Washington, D.C.: Government Printing Office, 1977).

Kirk, Paul L., "Human Hair Studies I: General Considerations of Hair Individualization and its Forensic Importance," Journal of Criminal Law and Criminology, 31:486, 1940.

Montagna, W. and Ellis, R.A., The Biology of Hair Growth, (New York: Academic Press, 1958).

Thornton, J.I. (Ed.), Crime Investigation, 2nd Edition, (New York: John Wiley and Sons, 1974).

"Don't Miss a Hair," FBI Law Enforcement Bulletin, May 1976.

SKINPRINTS, VOICEPRINTS, HANDWRITING

I. Skinprints

Skinprints include those areas on the human body where friction ridges are absent but sufficient skin patterns are present for individual identification. These areas include ears, lips, fingernails, and skin wrinkles/depression patterns. With the exception of earprints, little research has been conducted on the forensic value of lip prints, fingernail patterns and skin patterns. However, each of these areas have been utilized in criminal investigation for identification purposes.

In the 1950's Alfred Iannarelli developed a quantitative ear identification and classification system (1). Generally, courts will accept ear identification in the same manner as fingerprints. Ear identification refers to the external anatomy of the ear. Although the growth and aging process will change the size of the ear; the shape and proportion of the ear remains unchanged from infancy throughout life. The ear is made up of folded cartilage covered with skin that establishes several landmarks important in identification. Figure 22 shows these identification landmark areas.

Ear identification can be made from photographs or from developed latent prints of ears (such as from safe doors). Developing latent earprints at a crime scene is performed in the same manner as with fingerprints. For comparison purposes with latent earprints, photographs of the suspect's ear may be made although an ear impression is generally best. Ear impressions of a suspect should be made on a glass or metal slab then developed in the same manner as the latent earprint. One should not use fingerprint ink to take impressions of a suspect's ear.

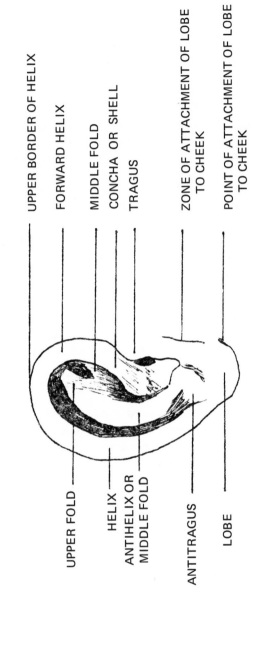

UPPER BORDER OF HELIX

FORWARD HELIX

MIDDLE FOLD

CONCHA OR SHELL

TRAGUS

ZONE OF ATTACHMENT OF LOBE
TO CHEEK

POINT OF ATTACHMENT OF LOBE
TO CHEEK

UPPER FOLD

HELIX

ANTIHELIX OR
MIDDLE FOLD

ANTITRAGUS

LOBE

FIGURE 22.   ANATOMY OF THE HUMAN EAR.

Lip prints may be found on cigarette butts, drinking utensils, cloth, tissue paper, etc. With the exception of a lipstick wearer, most lip prints are latent images. The use of latent fingerprint developing techniques have not proven useful in developing latent lip prints, due to the fact that lips do not possess pores that secrete oils and amino acids. However, some success has been found in the use of saliva tests to produce a visible lip print image. A ferric nitrate solution (5% w/v) may be used successfully to produce an orange-red color showing the lip print patterns. The ferric nitrate reacts with iron ions (thiocyanate ions) contained in human saliva (2:79). Patterns on lip prints are compared with known lip impressions in the same manner as fingerprints. As yet, there is no useful classification method for lip prints.

In some cases, investigators may find broken or cut fingernails or toenails at a crime scene. The microscopic growth striation markings in nails may be compared in the same manner as toolmarks or bullet identification.

There are several recorded cases which involve arm prints and knee prints left at a crime scene. Arm prints and knee prints produce individual skin patterning similar in appearance to alligator skin under a stereo microscope (40x). These patterns are compared with known impressions in the same manner as fingerprints or earprints.

II. Voiceprints

While voiceprints have not been as widely accepted as fingerprints, they do serve as a valuable means of human identification. The Bell Telephone Laboratories first produced the voice spectrograph during World War II as an aid to identify voices on enemy radios. Dr. L. G.

Kersta, of Bell Laboratories, improved the voiceprint spectrograph following the war and applied its use to criminal investigations (3:4-9).

The vocal mechanism of an individual provides the uniqueness upon which voiceprint identification is based. Sound consists, mainly, of pressure waves of varying frequencies and amplitudes. The vocal cavities of a human act as resonators, much like organ pipes. These vocal cavities cause sound energy to be reinforced in specific spectrum areas dependent upon the size of the vocal cavities. The major vocal cavities and the two oral cavities are formed in the mouth by positioning the tongue (Figure 23). The likelihood of two people having all vocal cavities the same size and coupled identically is remote. Other components of the speech process are the lips, teeth, tongue, soft palate, and jaw muscles. Their controlled interplay results in intelligible speech patterns. The manner in which the above articulators are manipulated during speech is distinctive to that one person.

Voiceprint identification utilizes a classification system like fingerprints. The ten most frequently used English words are used in the classification system: it, me, you, the, on, I, is, a, to. Voiceprints made of public figures from different stages of their careers were not shown to be significantly different (4). This would indicate that aging has little effect on the voice characteristics.

The voice spectrograph may produce two types of voiceprints. Bar voiceprints show voice resonance bars with dimensions of time, frequency, and loudness. Contour voiceprints measure levels of loudness, time, and frequency in a shape much like a topographical map (Figure 24).

Generally, voiceprint identification is useful only when the recorded voice of an unknown individual exists. Electronic eavesdropping,

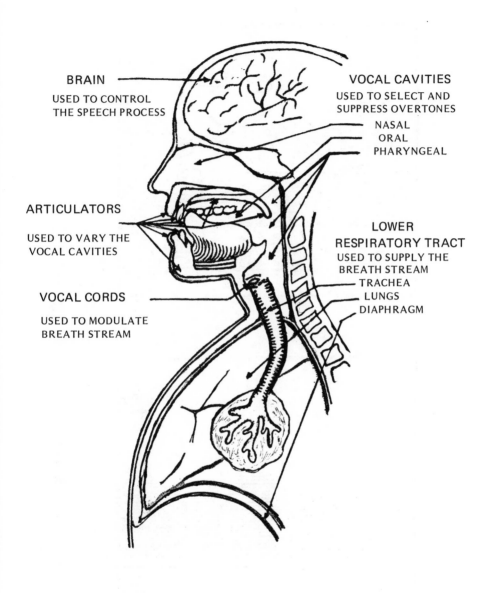

BRAIN

USED TO CONTROL
THE SPEECH PROCESS

VOCAL CAVITIES

USED TO SELECT AND
SUPPRESS OVERTONES

NASAL
ORAL
PHARYNGEAL

ARTICULATORS

USED TO VARY THE
VOCAL CAVITIES

**LOWER
RESPIRATORY TRACT**

USED TO SUPPLY THE
BREATH STREAM

TRACHEA
LUNGS
DIAPHRAGM

VOCAL CORDS

USED TO MODULATE
BREATH STREAM

FIGURE 23.   THE VOCAL MECHANISM.

FIGURE 24. BAR (left) AND CONTOUR (right) VOICEPRINTS.

threatening telephone calls, and radio transmissions of voices can be recorded and compared with the known voiceprints of a suspect for identification purposes (Figure 25). Numerous experiments have continued to prove that voiceprints are a positive means of identification even when compared with identical twins. It is believed that voiceprint identification accuracy lies somewhere between the present accuracy of fingerprints and handwriting.

III. Handwriting

The examination of questioned documents frequently include handwriting comparisons. Generally, handwriting comparisons may determine: 1) whether a document was written by a particular person; 2) whether a document was written by the same person whose signature it bears; 3) whether the writing has been altered for additions or deletions; and 4) whether a document has been forged. Comparing handwriting is similar in principle to fingerprint identification. No two products are identical, and differences can be perceived if a sufficiently close examination is made.

Children learn to write by copying letters that match a standard style. The United States uses either the Palmer system (1880) or the Zaner-Bloser system (1895). The student practicing handwriting makes a conscious effort to copy standard forms of letters. As writing skills increase, a child will reach a stage where the motor and nerve response associated with handwriting becomes a subconscious act. The individual's handwriting will take on shapes and patterns that will distinguish it from all others. The subconscious handwriting of two individuals can never be duplicated. The combination of physical, mental, and mechanical function of handwriting makes it extremely unlikely that variations in handwriting will be reproduced by two individuals (Figure 26).

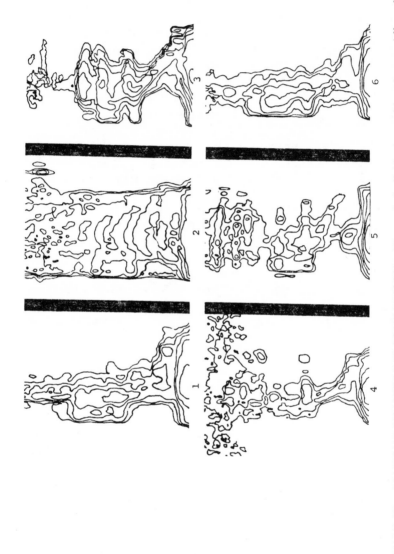

FIGURE 25. CONTOUR VOICEPRINT COMPARISON. Five male individuals speaking the word "you." Voiceprints 1 and 6 were spoken by the same person.

98

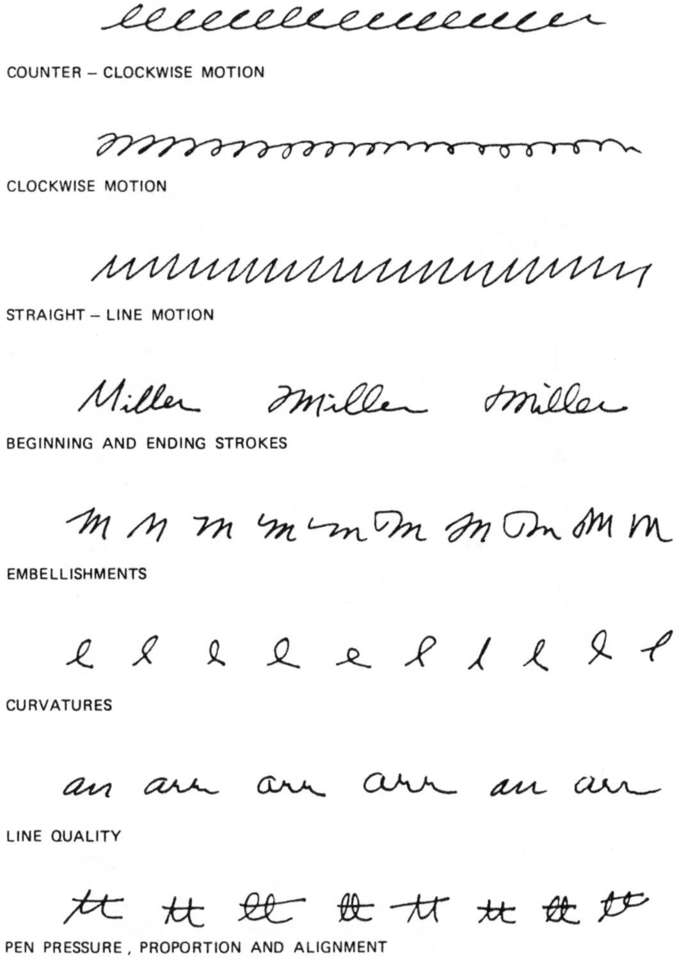

COUNTER – CLOCKWISE MOTION

CLOCKWISE MOTION

STRAIGHT – LINE MOTION

BEGINNING AND ENDING STROKES

EMBELLISHMENTS

CURVATURES

LINE QUALITY

PEN PRESSURE , PROPORTION AND ALIGNMENT

FIGURE 26.   CHARACTERISTIC HANDWRITING MOVEMENTS.

Forensic handwriting experts will examine four basic characteristics of handwriting for identification purposes:

1. Line Quality: The lines forming the letters will vary in visual appearance with respect to pen position, pressure, shading, tremor, rhythm, skill, speed, and continuity (Figure 27).

2. Form: In the formation of letters, slant, proportion, strokes, retracing, and separations will vary with different individuals.

3. Spacing: The separation of words, letters, and lines can be examined for consistency.

4. Spelling and Punctuation: Word usage, age, and education are determining factors.

Even when handwriting is disguised, forged, or written in the unaccustomed hand, identification can be made by experts. The elements of handwriting most often changed for disguise purposes are those which drastically affect the pictorial appearance of the writing. For instance, writing with the unaccustomed hand, increasing or decreasing the slope, using handprinting, use of large embellishments, formation of loops, base line arrangement, spacing, approach and terminal strokes, and capital letters are all frequently used in attempts to disguise handwriting. Most features altered are those that lend themselves well to modification or substitution such as circling dots and periods and changing the formation of numbers (7 to 7, etc.). Most attempts to disguise handwriting are neither consistent nor successful. It is usually best to look at lower case letter formations in suspected disguised handwriting. The lower case letters frequently used for disguise purposes are v, e, s, k, and t. Other lower case letters are not easily disguised in handwriting. The problem of handwriting

QUESTIONED. Above note was given to a bank clerk during a robbery.

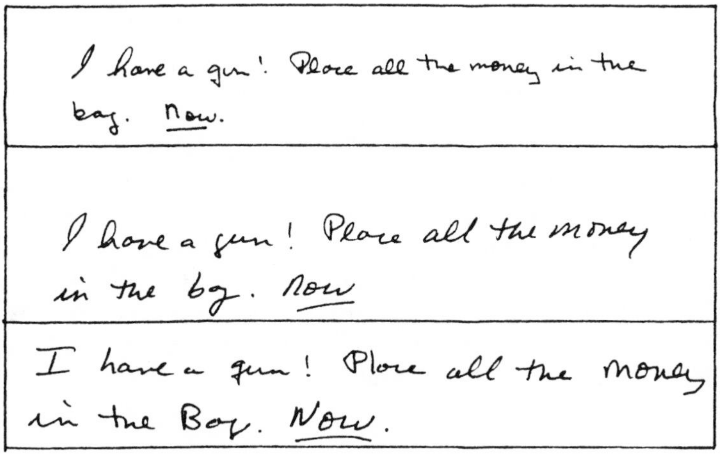

KNOWN. Above three known exemplars were written by the same individual during the course of an investigation. The suspect later plead quilty to the robbery. Notice the variations of the handwriting by the same person as well as the similarities.

FIGURE 27. COMPARISON OF KNOWN AND QUESTIONED HANDWRITING.

Other lower case letters are not easily disguised in handwriting. The problem of handwriting comparison comes from lack of a sufficient amount of questioned writing with which to compare with known standards (exemplars).

Handwriting exemplars are the actual and established handwriting samples written by a suspect for use as a basis for comparison. There are two types of exemplars:

1. <u>True standards:</u> Handwriting samples that were written in the due course of business (i.e., checks, contracts, letters, etc.).

2. <u>Request standards:</u> Those written by request on the witness stand or in the presence of law enforcement officers.

When obtaining request standard exemplars, the suspect should be required to write several examples including the same wording as the questioned document. In addition, the suspect should be required to write while standing, leaning, and sitting as the writing in these positions may vary. If the suspect is required to give sufficient exemplars, he/she will find difficulty in disguising the handwriting for comparison purposes (Figure 28).

IV. Steps For Obtaining Known Handwriting Exemplars

1. Before requested exemplars are taken from the suspect, a document examiner should be consulted and shown the questioned documents.

2. The writer should not be shown the questioned document or be provided with instructions on spelling or punctuation.

3. The suspect should be furnished a pen and paper similar to those used in the questioned document.

HANDWRITING EXEMPLAR FORM

Subject was: Sitting _____ Standing _____ Leaning _____ Case Number or Name _____

WRITE THE FOLLOWING:

Your Name _____

Street Address _____

City, State, Zip _____

Date of Birth _____ Age ____ Sex ____ Weight _____ Height _____ Hair Color ____ Eye Color ____

Adam C. Burling _____ A ____ R _____

Catherine E. Dolan _____ B ____ S _____

Edward H. Fallett _____ C ____ T _____

George K. Newburg _____ D ____ U _____

Mr. Levi Jacobson _____ E ____ V _____

Kitty M. Langdon _____ F ____ W _____

Margaret P. Hymans _____ G ____ X _____

Oliver R. Perper _____ H ____ Y _____

Quincy S. Roberts _____ I ____ Z _____

Stancil O. Torque _____ J ____ bb _____

Ulysses T. Velez _____ K ____ cc _____

Warren Bud Smith _____ L ____ dd _____

Cook F. Young, Jr. _____ M ____ pp _____

Ned Lee Harlow _____ N ____ tt _____

Harold I. Fox, Sr. _____ O ____ gg _____

Don V. Chesterfield _____ P ____ yy _____

1 2 3 4 5 6 7 8 9 0 _____ Q ____ ff _____

FIGURE 28a. HANDWRITING EXEMPLAR FORM.

HANDWRITING EXEMPLAR FORM

WRITE THE FOLLOWING: January _____ no _____

February _____ March _____ 100 _____

April _____ May _____ 00 _____

June _____ July _____ 16 _____

August _____ September _____ 17 _____

October _____ November _____ 22 _____

December _____ Seventeen _____ 33 _____

Nineteen _____ Cash _____ 556 _____

Dollars _____ Cents _____ 107 _____

and _____ Sixty-seven _____ 432 _____

Eighteen _____ Sixteen _____ 12 _____

Fourteen _____ Thirty-eight _____ 72 _____

Fifty-three _____ Ninety-six _____ 88 _____

Twelve _____ Forty-five _____ 192 _____

Fifteen _____ Thirteen _____ 98 _____

Seventy-two _____ One Hundred _____ 99 _____

Eleven _____ Ten _____ 876 _____

One Thousand _____ Twenty-two _____ no/100's _____

WRITE BELOW: The above samples of my handwriting written with my (right/left) hand. I normally
                write with my (right/left) hand.

_____

_____

_____

Witnessed (Initials) _____   Signed _____

_____   Date _____

FIGURE 28b.   HANDWRITING EXEMPLAR FORM.

4. The dictated text should be the same as the contents of the questioned documents, or at least should contain many of the same words, phrases, and letter combinations as found in the document. In handprinting cases, the suspect must not be given any instructions on using upper-case (capitals) or lower-case (small) lettering. If after writing several pages the writer fails to use the desired type of lettering, he can then be instructed to include it. Altogether, the text must be no shorter than a page.

5. Dictation of the text should take place at least three times. If the writer is making a deliberate effort to disguise his writing, noticeable variations should appear between the three repetitions.

References

1. Iannarelli, A.V., Iannarelli System of Ear Identification, (New York: The Foundation Press, 1964).

2. Miller, L.S., Brown, A.M., and Carimi, N.J. Criminal Evidence Laboratory Mannual: An Introduction to the Crime Laboratory, (Johnson City, TN: Institute of Social Sciences and Arts, Inc., 1985).

3. Kersta, L.G., "Voiceprint Identification," Identification News, December 1964, pp. 4-9.

4. Nash, E.W., and Tosi, O.I. "Identification of Suspects by the Voiceprint Technique," in Canoll R. Hormachea (Ed.), Sourcebook in Criminalistics, (Reston, VA: Reston Publishing Co., Inc., 1974).

Additional Reading

Anon, "Criminal Law-Evidence: Voiceprints Admissible to Corroborate Testimony, " Florida State University Law Review, 1:349, 1973.

Anon, "Voiceprint Identification: The Trend Towards Admissibility," New England Law Review, 9:419, 1974.

Baxter, P.G., "Handwriting: Principles and Practices," Criminologist, 25:11, 1972.

Bradford, R.R., "Obtaining Handwriting Exemplars from All Arrestees," Finger Print annd Identification Magazine, 6:3, 1973.

Brohier, Geoffry, "Document Examination," in Krishman, S.S. (Ed.), An Introduction to Modern Criminal Investigation, (Springfield, Illinois: Charles C. Thomas, 1978).

Brunelle, Richard L., "Questioned Document Examinations," in Saferstein, Richard (Ed.), Forensic Science Handbook, (Englewood Cliffs, New Jersey: Prentice-Hall, Inc., 1982).

Harrison, W.R., Suspect Documents: Their Scientific Examination (London: Sweet and Maxwell, 1958).

Iannarelli, A.V., Iannarelli System of Ear Identification, (New York: The Foundation Press, 1964).

Kersts, L.G., "Voiceprint Identification," Police Law Quarterly, 3:5, 1974.

Miller, L.S., Brown, A.M., and Carimi, N.J., Criminal Evidence Laboratory Manual: An Introduction to the Crime Laboratory, (Johnson City, TN: Institute of Social Sciences and Arts, Inc., 1985).

Miller, L.S., "Bias Among Forensic Document Examiners: A Need for Procedural Changes," <u>Journal of Police Science and Administration,</u> December, 1984.

Tosi, Oscar, <u>Voice Identification: Theory and Legal Applications,</u> (Baltimore: University Park Press, 1979).

On the Theory and Practice of <u>Voice Identification,</u> (Washington, D.C.: National Academy of Sciences, 1979).

6

POST-MORTEM INVESTIGATIONS

I. Investigation Of Death

Identifying deceased human remains is one of the first duties law enforcement personnel must perform in death cases. Obviously, the first duty of the law enforcement officer on arriving at the scene of an alleged fatal occurrence is to verify death. Police officers should not consider a person dead until the fact has been established by a competent individual (coroner, physician, etc.). In most states, the verification of death is made only by a licensed physician. In homicide cases, a physician, medical examiner or coroner should be summoned to the scene.

Definition of Death
_____

Generally, death is considered to have occurred when all these vital functions have irrevocably ceased: 1) respiration, 2) cardiac activity, and 3) central nervous system. Since 1972, brain death has been accepted as a legal definition of death (1). Brain death is the cessation of brain activity for 24 hours. In ordinary cases of death, the brain ceases to function when the heart and breathing ceases to function. However, with the technological advances of medical respirators to allow a patient's breathing to be maintained even when the brain is dead, the concept of brain death has become an important aspect of the definition of death. Recently, propositions have been made for all states to accept brain death as a legal definition of death.

Identification by Investigators
_____

The identification procedure begins with the criminal investigator's assignment to a death case. In most instances, a deceased human body can be easily identified. Relatives, friends, and acquaintances may all provide adequate identification. Missing and wanted person files can also be consulted in the identification process. Sometimes the identification of an unknown deceased person can be related to previous criminal convictions, property claims, insurance claims, desertion claims, and similar matters. The complete body discovered soon after death does not present any special problems for identification. Examination of clothes and possessions of the victim may provide clues to the identity of the individual. Decomposed, drowned, mutilated, or burned bodies may require the attention of experts.

The general procedure for identifying a dead body is similar to identifying living individuals. When the entire body has been discovered soon after death, the following identification procedures are recommended:

1. Determine if any witnesses were present. Relatives, friends, and acquaintances may have been with the person at the time of death or may have known where the person was. Visual identification can be made by these individuals.

2. Determine the physical description of the body. The same procedure here is not unlike portrait parle' for living individuals. The investigator should not be confused by body changes that are acquired after death, however. For example, swelling of the body may make the individual appear heavier; skin color changes may make the individual appear to be of a different race or appear to have birth marks or bruises on the body; the hair may change color (the investigator should also note that head hair is frequently dyed and a comparison should be made with hair on the body). The size of the clothing can aid in determining the weight and height of the individual if swelling has occurred.

110

3.   Obtain fingerprints of the deceased. This is the best means of identification since the fingerprints can be submitted to other law enforcement agencies (particularly the F.B.I.) with a request for a search of their files. A special apparatus is available for the taking of inked fingerprints from deceased bodies. This apparatus, a post-mortem fingerprint kit, does not require the rolling of fingers as the card holder is curved and can be pressed against the deceased's fingers. Even this procedure is sometimes difficult when rigor mortis has set into the body. When the fingers have been destroyed or mutilated by decay, drowning, or burning, specialized techniques must be employed and will be discussed in Chapter 7.

4.   Photographs should be taken of the whole body and head. Any unusual markings such as tatoos or scars should be photographed. Photographs may be shown to persons who may have known the deceased.

The medical examiner and/or coroner usually have the responsibility for a more detailed identification examination. These examinations generally involve the taking of blood and urine samples, hair samples, x-ray of the skeletal system, dental examinations, determination of time of death, and cause of death.

II. Changes In The Body After Death

When the three major systems of the human body ceases to function (circulatory, respiratory, and nervous), certain changes in the body will become apparent. One of the first changes after death is muscular flaccidity (relaxation). Contact flattening of the skin and pallor will be apparent when pressure is applied to the body. Later changes in the body permits an estimation of the time period which has elapsed since death. No exact time can be stated, only an interval in which death was likely to have occurred may be specified. This is known as the post-mortem interval. There are many factors that influence the estimation of this interval and should be considered in examining the body. Some of these factors include environmental temperature and humidity, location of the body, condition of the body at the time of death, etc. Immediately after death, the body will cool at the rate of approximately 1.5 degrees F. per hour until the environment temperature is reached (2). Obviously, the temperature of the environment will play an important role in the rate of temperature change of the body. In suspected homicide cases, the medical examiner or coroner at the scene should take the rectal or liver temperature of the body and the environment temperature as soon as possible, noting the time the readings were made. In addition, the age, size, amount of fat, clothing on the body, and position of the body will affect the rate of body cooling (Figure 29).

Livor Mortis

Livor mortis (also known as Post Mortem Lividity and Hypostasis) is the settling or pooling of body fluids due to gravity. Hence, if a person were lying on his back at the time of death, the body fluids would settle down toward the back.

The process begins immediately after death and becomes visually apparent 20-30 minutes after death. It appears as dull red patches which deepen in color and intensity within 6-10 hours. Small bluish-black hemorrhages may appear due to the rupture of engorged blood vessels. After 4-5 days, livor mortis becomes permanent or "fixed".

For forensic purposes, livor mortis can determine the posture of a body after death if the body has remained in one position for at least 10 hours after death. If livor mortis is not "fixed", movement of the body can redistribute body fluids into the new body position.

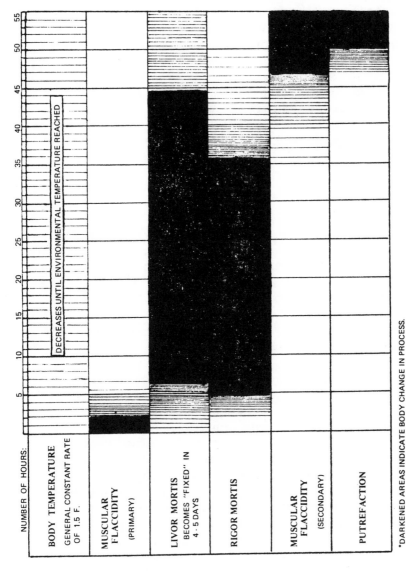

FIGURE 29. RATE OF PHYSICAL CHANGES AFTER DEATH.

*DARKENED AREAS INDICATE BODY CHANGE IN PROCESS.

The color of livor mortis may have a bearing on the cause of death. Usually the color is a reddish-purple. In carbon monoxide poisoning, the livor mortis will appear cherry red or pink due to carbon monoxide concentration in the blood. Livor mortis will also appear pink if the body has been in a cold environment.

Because livor mortis gives the appearance of a bruise, close observation should be made to differentiate bruises from livor mortis. In most instances, this can be determined by the medical examiner at autopsy.

Rigor Mortis

Rigor mortis is the stiffening of muscles due to chemical changes involving proteins of the muscle fibers. Every muscle in the body (both voluntary and involuntary) undergoes rigor mortis after death. The forcible bending of joints when rigor mortis is fully developed in skeletal muscles will tear the muscle fibers and the stiffening will not return.

Ordinarily, rigor mortis appears in 2-4 hours but can come as early as 30 minutes after death or as late as 6 hours or more. The higher the temperature of the environment the sooner rigor mortis develops. This is also dependent upon the clothing and body size of the deceased. Rigor mortis takes place in the body muscles at the same time. Rigor mortis appears to begin in the head muscles since smaller masses of muscle fibers are noticeably stiffer than larger masses of muscle fiber. This gives the appearance of the spreading of rigor mortis from head to toe. After many hours in rigor mortis the muscles soften due to putrefaction and muscle flaccidity (or secondary flaccidity) begins to set in. The environment and climate vary the time of disappearance of rigor mortis but, generally, secondary flaccidity begins 36-38 hours after death.

In some cases a false rigor mortis can result in a deceased body. There are three conditions which can simulate rigor mortis:

1. Cadaveric spasm - (Instantaneous Rigor) - is a form of muscular stiffening that occurs at the moment of death and persists until true rigor mortis develops. Its cause is unknown, but is usually associated with violent deaths in circumstances of intense emotion. Fatigue may also be a factor. Cadaveric spasm is an uncommon occurrence and should not be diagnosed unless the grasp of hands is tightly holding some article (i.e., weapons, hair, etc.). It is impossible to force a dead hand to grasp an article tightly.

2. Heat Stiffening - this will occur if the body is exposed to intense heat such as burning or immersion in hot liquid. It is the result of coagulation (drying) of the muscle proteins.

3. Cold Stiffening - any reduction in the temperature of a dead body below 40 degrees F. (3-5 degrees C.) will produce a notable stiffening of fat and muscle tissues. A cold environment will delay the development of true rigor mortis.

Putrefaction

The environment and temperature play important roles in the rate of decay of a dead body. There are two processes which causes a dead body to decay:

1. Autolysis - this is the softening of body tissues caused by the digestive action of enzymes which are released by body cells after death. Autolysis can be prevented only by freezing body tissues.

2. Bacterial action - bacteria which normally inhabit a body will begin to invade body

115

tissues upon death. Most bacteria come from the intestinal regions of the body. The blood provides an excellent medium for bacterial growth. It should be noted that putrefaction can be especially rapid if death was due to a bacterial disease.

Autolysis and bacterial action may begin immediately after death. However, visible signs of putrefaction first appear as a greenish discoloration of the abdomen on the second or third day after death. This is followed by discoloration over the chest and trunk of the body at the end of the first week of death. In addition, a foul odor of decay will be apparent. By the end of the first week of death some of the veins beneath the skin will be visible as a purplish-brown network. The outer layers of skin will begin to loosen and can be easily rubbed off. This is known as "skin slippage". By the second week of death, blisters filled with a watery fluid will form just beneath the skin. The trunk of the body will begin bloating with gas formation which may force fluid from the mouth and nose. By the third or fourth week of death, the hair, fingernails, and toenails can be easily pulled loose from the skin. The face will have a greenish-purple discoloration and will be bloated. The bloated face will be characterized by puffy cheeks, thick swollen lips and tongue, and the eyes swollen closed. The trunk of the body will also become bloated and swollen which may exaggerate the true body build. A deceased body, in this state of decay, will be difficult for a relative to identify. The organs of the body may shrink during the decomposition process, but can be identified for several months after death. This is particularly helpful when attempting to determine the sex of a decayed individual.

The timing of putrefaction cannot be done with accuracy. There are many variables which may increase the rate of decay or slow the decay process significantly. The most important element in the decay rate is temperature. Generally, the

116

warmer the temperature of a body and its environment, the faster the rate of decomposition. Bacterial action increases with warmer temperatures. The location of the body, amount of clothing on the body, position of the body, moisture, environmental temperatures and air flow are all important factors which can significantly change the rate of decay of a dead body. A body located in a warm, dry environment with little air movement may become mummified. Outside body tissues tend to dry and shrink rapidly in such an environment before decomposition. A dead body underwater will decay slower than one on the ground due to the colder temperatures and lack of oxygen.

Animals and insects will attack and feed upon a dead body depending on the environment, temperatures, and accessability. Flies may lay eggs in the corners of the eyes, nostrils, and lips within a few hours of death. Maggots may be visible as soon as twenty-four hours after death. Different species of insects are attracted to a dead body depending upon the freshness of the meat. As long as the environmental temperature remains above 40 degrees F. and the body is accessible, insects will feed upon the body. In some cases, entomologists may aid the investigator in determining the time since death based on insect activity. Figure 30 is an example of a checklist that may be used at the scene of a death where insects have invaded the body.

Rodents will also attack a dead body within a few hours of death. The absence of rodent attacks on a dead body in areas where rodents are known to exist is good indication that the body has been dead or has been moved to that location only a few hours before discovery. Birds, dogs, cats and other animals have all been known to eat and carry away portions of a dead body.

Determining the time of death is a difficult task, particularly when the body has begun the decomposition process. The medical examiner may be able to bracket the time of death based on the

117

ENTOMOLOGY REPORT FOR HUMAN DEATH SCENE

MEDICAL EXAMINER'S NAME:

ADDRESS:

IDENTIFYING CASE NUMBER :

INSECT CHECKLIST:

1. Insects were found:

___ a. In open wound on surface of body.
___ b. Around and in natural body openings on surface of body (i.e., eyes, nose, mouth, etc.).
___ c. Deep in body.
___ d. Under body.

2. Body was found:

___ a. Inside a buidling or shelter.
___ b. In heavy brush.
___ c. In an open field.
___ d. In a very moist area.
___ e. In a very dry area.
___ f. Uncovered.

3. Temperature at scene: _____ (indicate F. or C.).

4. Time at which temperature was recorded: _____ .

5. Range of temperatures for previous two weeks should be obtained from local weather bureau (attach to this list if possible).

6. Largest and smallest of each type of immature insect present should be collected and placed in 70% alcohol.

7. At least 30 of each type of immature insect should be put in separate jars with meat or small piece of muscle from victim. Meat must be replaced as it is consumed. Use at least a 16 oz. jar. Open jar periodically to air out. If maggots start to crawl out -- jar is too crowded, put some into another jar.

8. Collect and place adult insects in jar with cyanide if possible.

FIGURE 30.   ENTOMOLOGIST'S REPORT FORM.

general physical changes that have taken place. Again, such an estimation can only be made when the medical examiner has sufficient information about the environment in which the body was discovered (i.e., temperature, clothing, position of the body, etc.). In most cases a soft, white, greasy material will form on the soft tissues of a decaying body. This material is known as adipocere formation. Adipocere formation begins within days of death if a body is exposed to a moist environment. Adipocere formation is caused by the fatty acids in the body and is most visible on the cheeks of the face, buttocks, and breasts of a deceased individual. The patchy adipocere formation tends to preserve the features of the body up to several weeks after death which is helpful in the identification of the body and the determination of the cause of death. Running water and a cold temperature retards adipocere formation. Adipocere formation is typically seen in geographic areas where humidity is high.

III. Role Of The Medical Examiner And Forensic Pathologist

Law enforcement agencies often utilize the services of three different specialists during the investigation of a death. These three specialists (coroner, medical examiner, and forensic pathologist) are somewhat similar in duties but may vary considerably.

The coroner and the medical examiner are, in most states, the same person. In some states, however, the coroner is a politically appointed or elected position in the county government. Political coroners usually have little medical training and their duties in death investigations are limited to the pronunciation of death at the scene, collection of blood and urine samples from the deceased, and assistance to the medical examiner (a physician).

The medical examiner is almost always a physician, and is generally contracted for the position by the state or county health department. The duties of the medical examiner include examination of wounds suffered on and within a deceased's body, determination of the mode of death (autopsy), identification of the deceased, measurement of wounds (point of entry, exit, angle, etc.), and the determination of length of time since death (post mortem interval).

The role of the forensic pathologist is nearly the same as that of the medical examiner. In discussing the roles of the coroner, medical examiner, and forensic pathologist, it should be noted that they are not mutually exclusive. For instance, a forensic pathologist may serve as the medical examiner and/or coroner.

The forensic pathologist, after obtaining a doctor of medicine degree, is trained further in the field of forensic pathology. This training lends itself more readily to the law enforcement field than does the training of a physician. The role of the forensic pathologist is that of a specialist concerning knowledge of factors in medico-legal cases (i.e., homicides). Quite often, the forensic pathologist makes significant contributions to the investigation and conclusion of death investigations encountered by law enforcement agencies. He may determine the cause of death, identity of the deceased, time of death, manner of death, weapon used (mechanism of death), and provide expert testimony in court.

Post-Mortem Examinations

As a general rule, a post-mortem examination and autopsy should be performed in every unnatural death. In particular, violent deaths, accidental deaths, suicides, sudden deaths where the person has been in apparent good health, deaths unattended by a physician, prison deaths, and suspicious or unusual deaths should all be subject to post-mortem examinations.

A physician, medical examiner, or coroner should go to the scene of death to take charge of a dead body (in some states this is required by law). Obviously, if there is any doubt that a person is not dead, they should be taken immediately to a hospital. It is always good practice for the medical examiner or coroner to be called to the scene. Both the medical examiner and investigating police officers may work together to reconstruct the crime scene, determine the post-mortem interval, and discover evidence that may be overlooked.

When the body is removed from the scene, it should be taken to a morgue facility. The transportation of the body must be carefully done so that soiling of the deceased's clothing and loss of evidence such as hairs and fibers does not occur. The body should not be handled roughly so as to create new injuries or disturb existing wounds which would be difficult to determine at the autopsy. The hands of the deceased should be "bagged" with common paper sacks to prevent contamination or loss of physical evidence. Do not use plastic bags as plastic will create moisture that may destroy evidence.

Law enforcement investigators do not engage in autopsy work themselves. They are, however, expected to assist the medical examiner during the procedure. The investigator should determine that the medico-legal purposes of the autopsy are being performed (governed by the rules of evidence). The investigator should make sure that all physical evidence (such as bullets, semen, hairs, etc.) are properly extracted and preserved for further analysis as evidence.

Autopsy Procedures

An autopsy (also known as a necropsy) is a systematic fixed routine of dissection of a body.

The examination is not limited to the region where the cause of death was supposedly incurred. The customary procedure of an autopsy is:

1. Weigh and measure the body and record the dimensions and sites of all external changes such as wounds (Figure 31).

2. Collect particles of material from the body surface and from the nails. Fingernails should be clipped and placed in labeled envelopes. Never scrape fingernails. Collect body hair from various areas. Hair should be pulled, not cut, and placed in labeled envelopes.

3. Examine the perineum in a good light. Take samples. Examine the inside of the lips.

4. Determine temperature, rigor and hypostasis.

5. Take x-ray photographs where indicated.

6. Always consider the possibility of air or fat embolism.

7. Dissect systematically. The head and brain, thorax, abdomen, pelvis, extremities, and various regions.

8. Collect all body fluids, including bile.

9. Take swabs for microbiology.

10. Weigh all organs, measure all wounds and determine their relationship to fixed sites on the external surface.

11. Dictate a report (known as autopsy protocol).

12. Make a final examination of the external features to ensure that nothing has been missed.

WHEN DESCRIBING A HUMAN BODY FOR MEDICAL EXAMINER PURPOSES OR FOR WRITTEN REPORTS, IT IS RECOMMENDED TO USE PROPER MEDICAL TERMS FOR THE AREAS OF THE HUMAN BODY. THE DIAGRAM BELOW DEPICTS THE AREAS OF A HUMAN BODY COMMONLY USED IN MEDICAL AND FORENSIC SCIENCE IN—VESTIGATION REPORTS.

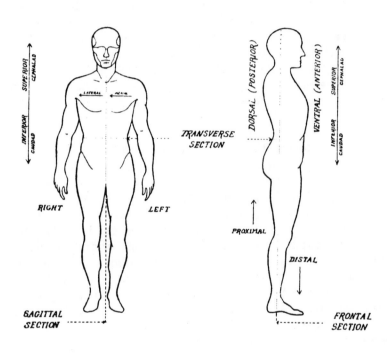

FIGURE 31. HUMAN BODY DESCRIPTION.

123

The medical examiner should always note anomalies, marks and scars, wounds, and foreign matter. These should be measured, photographed and/or collected (dissected out) for further analysis (Figure 32).

The medical examiner should also assist in the identification of unknown bodies. Depending upon his/her experience and skill, the medical examiner may be able to supply a detailed description of a person from a decomposed body. X-rays may reveal healed fractures and dissection may reveal previous surgery that may aid in the identification process. In badly burned or advanced decomposed bodies, dental experts and forensic anthropologists may be required to describe and help identify the deceased individual.

IV. Role Of The Police Investigator At Autopsy

Police investigators should always attend the autopsy in suspicious and unnatural death investigations. The purpose is twofold: first, the investigator may aid the medical examiner with information regarding the crime scene, evidence, environmental conditions, etc., which in turn may lead to a more conclusive determination of the cause, manner, and mechanism of death; secondly, the investigator may extract physical evidence for submission to a crime laboratory and may learn immediate results without waiting for an autopsy protocol. The following list details the role of the police investigator at autopsy:

1. Attend all autopsies in unnatural, suspect death investigations.

2. Take detailed notes, keeping in mind the rules of evidence and the establishment of elements of a criminal offense for prosecution purposes.

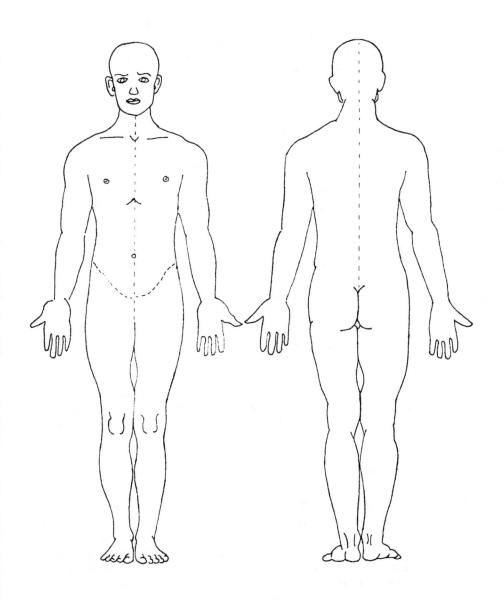

FIGURE 32. TYPICAL BODY DIAGRAM CHART USED BY MEDICAL
EXAMINERS.

3.   Make photographs of important areas on the
body (e.g., death wounds, tatoos, scars,
defensive wounds, hesitation wounds in
suicides, etc.).

4.   Collect all clothing and personal items of
the deceased for inventory and lab analysis.

5.   Make sure the medical examiner takes blood,
urine, and body fluid evidence for
pathological examination (e.g., drug screen,
toxic substances, alcohol).

6.   Collect samples of head hair and pubic hair
(pluck, do not cut at least 20 hairs from
each region).

7.   Collect fingernail snippings (do not scrape)
from the deceased's hands for submission to a
crime laboratory.

8.   If available, bring suspected death
instruments (e.g., knives, hatchets, guns,
etc.) to the autopsy for immediate comparison
with wounds and consultation with the
medical examiner.

9.   In cases of firearm wounds, examine and
photograph external powder residue patterns
for distance determination. Do the same with
the clothing of the deceased.

10.   Examine the hands for gun powder residue in
suspected firearms deaths. Take swabbings
for laboratory analysis (Neutron Activation
Analysis or Atomic Absorption Analysis).

11.   Collect all physical evidence from the body
for submission to the crime laboratory (e.g.,
bullets, foreign hair and fiber, plant
material, soil, etc.).

12.   Supervise the medical examiner in
presentation of evidence during the autopsy

to prevent the destruction of physical evidence.

13. Take fingerprints of the deceased if unidentified.

14. Conduct field tests on the skin of the deceased where appropriate (e.g., trace metal detection on hands).

One cannot stress the importance of the presence of police investigators at autopsies. Most medical personnel are untrained in the investigation of homicides and suicides and, therefore, may unknowingly destroy evidence or fail to make appropriate examinations. Many police investigators incorrectly assume that such examinations will be performed or that the medical examiner is trained in such investigations. Once the body has been interred or cremated, the investigator will rarely have a secord chance to perform such examinations. The investigator should bring the following items with him/her to an autopsy:

1. Notepad and pencil.

2. Camera with color slide film and infrared film (infrared for gun powder residue detection).

3. Post-mortem fingerprint kit.

4. Petri dishes, plastic envelopes, paper bags, and various glass containers for collection of evidence (e.g., bullets, hair, fiber, soil, etc.).

5. Fingernail clippers and small paper envelopes (be sure to label which finger and hand the clippings came from).

6. Trace metal detection kit to determine if metal touched the hands or other parts of the body.

127

7. Gun powder residue kit to determine if
    nitrates are present on hands or other parts
    of the body.

All physical evidence collected should be labeled
with the date and time of autopsy, the physician's
name and the investigator making the collection.
These items of physical evidence should be
submitted to a crime laboratory with the
appropriate request for anlalysis.

Trace Metal Detection

        A very useful kit at autopsies to determine
if a deceased individual has grasped a metal
object (e.g., firearms) is the Trace Metal
Detection kit (TMD). There are two chemical test
kits that can be inexpensively prepared for TMD:
1) the 8-Hydroxyquinoline test; and, 2) the
Ferrozine test.

        The 8-Hydroxyquinoline test is conducted by
preparing a 0.1% to 0.2% solution of 8-
Hydroxyquinoline in isopropanol. The reagent is
sprayed onto the hands and, if the deceased
recently held a metal object, the reagent reacts
with traces of metallic oxide deposits on the
hands. Short-wave ultraviolet illumination will
reveal charactistic colors for different metals:

        steel and iron: black, purple
        brass and copper: purple
        aluminum: mottled dull yellow
        lead: tarnish flesh color

        The Ferrozine method is used for steel and
iron deposits only. This test is conducted by
mixing a 0.1% solution of ferrozine in methanol.
The reagent is also commonly known as PDT (3-(2-
pyridyl)-5, 6-diphenyl-1, 2, 4-triazine-p, p1-
disulphonic acid, disodium salt trihydrate). The
reagent is sprayed onto the deceased's hands and,
if the subject held a steel or iron object

recently, a red colored stain will appear within one minute under visible light.

The use of either test will conclusively confirm whether a deceasd individual held or grasped a firearm. Such tests are particularly useful in firearm suicide determinations.

Gun Powder Residues

The investigator should swab the deceased's hands with a cotton swab soaked with acetone for crime laboratory examination to determine if gunpowder residues (nitrates, barium, nickel, lead, antimony, etc.) are present. Such examinations at a crime laboratory may be beneficial to determine if the deceased fired a weapon. The investigator should remember that only crime laboratories equipped with Atomic Absorption or Neutron Activation Analysis (requires a nuclear reactor) can conclusively make such determinations.

The clothing of the deceased should be submitted to a crime laboratory to determine bullet holes and powder patterns for distance determination. The suspected weapon (if available) should also be submitted for test firings to determine distance patterns of residues.

At autopsy, the investigator should photograph and measure the distribution of powder residues around the bullet wound. It is important that this examination be made before the body is cleaned and/or dissected. In cases where the skin around the bullet hole is blood soaked or in cases where the skin is too dark to determine powder residues (e.g., negroid subjects), the wound area should be photographed with black and white infrared film using a Kodak Wratten number 87 filter (ASA 100). The infrared image will omit unwanted contrast of skin tones and blood (2:131).

References

1. Camps, Francis E., _Gradwohl's Legal Medicine,_ 3rd Edition, (Chicago: Year Book Medical Publications, Inc., 1976), p. 51, 97.

2. Miller, L.S., Brown, A.M., and Carimi N.J., _Criminal Evidence Laboratory Manual: An Introduction to the Crime Laboratory._ (Johnson City, TN: Institute of Social Sciences and Arts, Inc., 1985), p. 131.

Additional Readings

Adelson, L., The Pathology of Homicide, (Springfield, Illinois: Charles C. Thomas, 1974).

Camps, Francis (Ed.), _Gradwohl's Legal Medicine,_ 3rd Edition, (Chicago: Year Book Medical Publications, Inc., 1976).

Francisco, J.T., "Law Enforcement and the Forensic Pathologist," _FBI Law Enforcement Bulletin,_ February, 1973.

Hendrix, R.C., _Investigation of Sudden and Violent Death,_ (Springfield, Illinois: Charles C. Thomas, 1972).

Miller, L.S., Brown, A.M., and Carimi, N.J., _Criminal Evidence Laboratory Manual: An Introduction to the Crime Laboratory._ (Johnson City, TN: Institute of Social Sciences and Arts, Inc., 1985).

Moritz, A.R. and Morris, R.D., _Handbook of Legal Medicine,_ 3rd Edition, (New York: Mosby, 1970).

Sopher, I.M., "The Law Enforcement Officer and the Determination of the Time of Death," _FBI Law Enforcement Bulletin,_ October, 1973.

IDENTIFYING HUMAN REMAINS

I. Fingerprinting Deceased Individuals

When an investigator is confronted with the task of fingerprinting a dead body, he must consider the condition of the corpse. In certain cases, the amputation of the hands for laboratory examination may be necessary. The medical examiner or surgeon may perform the operation and legal authority must be obtained in advance (1). Generally, the investigator should base his judgment upon the fragility of the skin on fingers. Photography should be used before any attempt is made to fingerprint a dead body. Close-up photographs of the fingers can be used for identification purposes if the fingerprints are destroyed in the printing process.

Recently Dead

If death occurred within the previous ten hours and rigor mortis has not set in, the following procedure may be used:

1. Use a post-mortem fingerprint kit which contains a set of fingerprint card strips (these may be cut from standard 8x8 fingerprint cards), an inking slab, and a curved fingerprint strip (card) holder (also known as a "spoon"). With this apparatus, rolling the fingers is unnecessary and the effect of rolled finger impressions is achieved by pressing the finger against the spoon. The entire pattern can be obtained in this manner.

2. The arms of the deceased should be extended forward and fingers inked with the ink slab.

3. If the fingers of the deceased are clenched, they can be extended by standing behind the

deceased's shoulders and lifting the arms as to extend them above the head. Massaging the hands or soaking them in warm water can also relax the fingers.

4. If the fingers are wrinkled from immersion in liquid, it may be necessary to fill out the fingers before a satisfactory impression can be made. The use of a hypodermic needle filled with warm water, glycerin, or other suitable liquid may be used to inject under the first joint of the finger. By injecting the liquid, the normal contour of the finger can be restored. A piece of string may be used to tie around the finger above the injection hole to prevent fluid from escaping.

Decomposed Bodies

Again, photographs should be made with careful lighting to give detail to the ridges. The fingers should be cleaned with water or xylene, then inked and printed in the usual manner. The outer skin or epidermis may be destroyed in some cases. The second layer of skin has a less pronounced ridge detail but satisfactory prints can be obtained if the investigator is careful. In some cases the skin may have to be removed by cutting the fingerprint from the finger. The operator places the removed skin over his own finger (protected by a rubber glove) and prints as though it were his own finger. The skin may also be placed on a smooth surface and photographed. The removal of skin is a frequent necessity in drowning cases. For fine or worn ridge detail, the dusting-tape method may yield excellent results and may be superior to inked impressions. Ordinary black fingerprint dusting powder is applied to the fingers (first cleaned with water or xylene) using a fingerprint brush or cotton ball. A piece of fingerprint tape is then applied to the dusted ridges of each finger, peeled off and placed against a piece of glass or other transparent material (viewing from the other side for comparison with inked prints).

II. Locating Buried Bodies

It is not uncommon for a law enforcement agency to conduct searches for buried human bodies. The law enforcement officer investigating a homicide in which the victim was buried should make every attempt to obtain as much information about the burial site as possible. It is helpful to know whether the death occurred at the burial site or elsewhere. Most individuals are not capable of carrying or dragging a body any great distance; therefore, the grave usually will be close (i.e., approximately 50 feet) to a highway or an area accessible by a motor vehicle. If the homicide was committed at the burial site, the grave will be in a more isolated spot further from highways and residences. Victims are usually forced to walk to an isolated area where shots or screams will not be heard.

Searching for a buried body is usually not an emergency situation, therefore, there is time for a thorough search. The weather bureau may be able to advise what weather conditions have existed in the search area which could help determine soil conditions and vegetation growth. Searching for buried bodies is similar to outside crime scene search techniques. A detailed map and/or aerial photograph of the area to be searched is very useful in laying out search patterns. In any case, photograph the area as thoroughly as possible. Photographs will not only be helpful in determining landmarks for site location, but will be useful in court to indicate relationships to physical evidence. The area to be searched should be marked off by boundaries and a grid pattern should be no larger than law enforcement personnel can search in one day. Using a grid pattern will help eliminate the chances of some of the area not being covered during the search.

There are three methods of searching for buried bodies: 1) visual searches; 2) aerial searches; and 3) probe searches. The visual searches and aerial searches are the most expedient methods. The probe search is time consuming, but will give indications not available with visual or aerial searches.

Visual Searches

Visual searches generally incorporate the determination of "disturbed ground area". When a body is buried there will be telltale signs of soil disturbance. During digging, soil will normally be placed on one side of the hole or the other. While the soil is being piled, any vegetation growing next to the grave will be damaged and soil intermixed with the vegetation. Another indication of disturbed areas is soil compaction or depressions. Each type of soil has a different rate of compaction, therefore, the depth of the depression may vary with different soils and moisture content. A depression may occur by soil settling into the abdominal cavity as the body decays. This depression is called "secondary depression". A secondary depression will normally occur on graves less than thirty inches in depth.

Aerial Searches

The main advantage of aerial searches is the fact that large areas can be covered in the minimal amount of time with a minimum of personnel. Suspected burial sites can be located from the air and transmitted to ground crews. In addition, aerial photographs can be made of the area. Forested land or areas with great vegetation growth may hinder aerial searches. However, a decaying body may supply more nutrients to vegetation immediately over the grave leading to more lush vegetation. Lush vegetation is more easily seen in dryer arid areas.

The use of infrared film in aerial searches may prove useful if the grave is shallow and fresh. Infrared photography has not been successful in detecting graves over forty eight hours old, however (2).

Probe Searches

If visual and/or aerial searches prove unsuccessful, the use of probes becomes necessary. A probe is a metal rod approximately four feet long, with a wooden handle at one end. The other end consists of a sharp point with a groove running down the middle (2). By sticking the rod into the ground and making a 180 degree twist, the soil will adhere in the groove of the rod. The probe is used to sample layers of soil in a given area. These probes are used by agricultural chemists to test the quality of soil and the properties of various fertilizers.

The areas to be probe searched should use the grid system, and personnel using probes should be formed in a line moving forward at two foot intervals. Probes should look for "soft spots" indicative of disturbed soil and decaying matter. Although soft spots occur from vegetation decomposition or burrowing animals, the samples of soil material brought up in the probe rod groove may indicate a decaying body. Human body decomposition produces a high percentage of alkaline substances and acids from the breakdown of albuminous tissues and sugar decomposition. Such alkalines and acids will produce a strong reaction to litmus paper. Therefore, when a soft spot is located, the soil samples in the groove of the probe can be tested with litmus paper to determine body decomposition. In most cases the tip end of the rod will have the characteristic odor of a decaying body.

Gas vapor detection equipment used in safety inspection for industry may also prove useful in locating buried bodies with a probe. After a body is buried for a period of time, decomposition of tissues forms the gases hydrogen sulfide, hydrogen phosphate, carbon dioxide, methane, ammonia, and hydrogen. The gas sensing probe is inserted into the probe hole for temperature readings and to determine the presence of gases being produced by a decaying body. Such gas detection instruments can also be used to search areas covered by concrete or asphalt by drilling small holes through the surface and inserting the gas probe. Gas detection equipment has been known to detect the presence of a body decaying for over ten years.

III. Excavating Buried Bodies

Once the outline of the grave has been determined, it is necessary to carefully remove the soil within the grave outline. The use of mechanical digging devices is discouraged because of the destructiveness of the devices. The objective of exhumation is to reconstruct the events of the burial. Articles of clothing, discarded items by the perpetrator, and other pieces of evidence are as important as the removal of the body. No bone or part of the body should be removed until the entire grave has been exposed. The use of digging trowels and brushes will expose a body and any other artifacts in their original position. It is important to make photographs and take measurements of body position in relation to other landmarks. Once the body or skeleton has been removed, care should be taken to search the soil below and around the edge of the body or skeleton. Bullets fired into the body may be found in this associated soil.

If the body has flesh still adhering to the bones, a "body bag" should be used to pack and transport the body to the morgue. If the body has completely decomposed, the bones may be packaged in separate containers. Large bones should be packed separately from smaller ones to prevent breakage in transport. Each container should be labeled carefully.

IV. Forensic Odontology

Forensic odontology is concerned with the identification of human individuals based on dental examination. Dental evidence for identification purposes is important because teeth and teeth supporting bone (alveolar process) are characteristic of an individual. In addition, teeth are more indestructible than any other body tissue, as are some of the materials utilized for dentures and restorations. Bitemarks left in various substances may reveal individual dental features that make identification of the teeth of the perpetrator possible.

When deceased individuals cannot be positively identified through fingerprints, facial characteristics, tatoos, hair or skin color because of body decomposition, mutilation, or burning, dental structures become one of the few means by which a binding legal identification can be attained. However, law enforcement officials must have the name and dental records of the suspected individual with which to compare dental findings.

Human Dentition

Under normal conditions, the upper and lower jaws of an individual will contain the same number and types of teeth. Adult dentition is expressed in the following dental formula:

Upper Right:	32 12	21 23	Upper Left
Lower Right:	32 12	21 23	Lower Left

There are a total of 32 adult teeth. Reading from the center of the formula outward they are: two incisors, one canine, two premolars, and three molars.

There are a total of 20 deciduous teeth (baby or milk teeth). The formula for deciduous teeth is:

Upper Right:	212	212	Upper Left
Lower Left:	212	212	Lower Left

or, two incisors, one canine, and two premolars (Figure 33).

Dental Identification

A complete detailed examination should be performed by a dentist specifically trained in the collection and handling of dental evidence. The examination should include: 1) charting; 2) x-rays; 3) model construction; 4) determination of age based on dentition; and 5) examination of any dentures, tooth fragments, or suspected tooth fragments found separated from the body. In some cases, it may be necessary to remove the jaws for examination.

Dental charting, x-ray records, models and indications of dental work performed on the unknown body may be compared to dental records of missing persons for a possible match. The success of this procedure depends upon the accuracy of dental records kept by dental surgeons. Dental X-rays (also called "radiographs") are of prime importance since they offer means of obtaining a positive identification when compared with x-rays of missing individuals (3).

Age Determination

The approximate age of a deceased individual based on dentition may be determined at the preliminary examination. This will help to narrow the number of suspected missing persons to an age group. The chronology of tooth development in children has been studied extensively. There are a number of methods which may determine the approximate age of a deceased child. Cross-

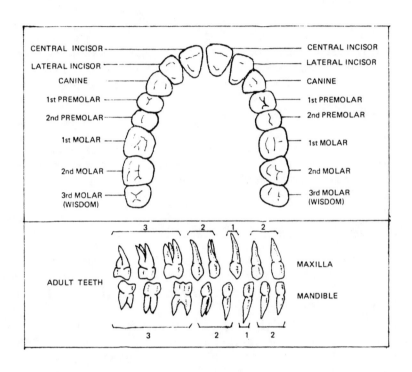

CENTRAL INCISOR
LATERAL INCISOR
CANINE
1st PREMOLAR
2nd PREMOLAR
1st MOLAR
2nd MOLAR
3rd MOLAR (WISDOM)

CENTRAL INCISOR
LATERAL INCISOR
CANINE
1st PREMOLAR
2nd PREMOLAR
1st MOLAR
2nd MOLAR
3rd MOLAR (WISDOM)

ADULT TEETH

MAXILLA

MANDIBLE

FIGURE 33. HUMAN DENTITION.

sections of enamel on children's teeth have been suggested as a means of indicating increments of growth (4). Mixed dentition (when permanent teeth and baby teeth are both present) is also a means of establishing age. When identifying adult bodies, it is necessary to apply other means of age estimation. The adult tooth goes through progressive changes that may be correlated with known populations in order to estimate age. Dental changes suggested for such identification examinations include 1) attrition (wearing away of teeth in the course of normal wear); 2) paradentosis (degeneration of tissues and bone supporting the teeth); 3) secondary dentin (new dentin formed in response to normal aging process); 4) cementum (bonelike connective tissue covering the root of the tooth which is calcified and arranged in layers); 5) root resorption (loss of dentin cementum or alveolar process); and 6) root transparency.

Post-Mortem Dental Examination

The post-mortem dental examination and charting of unidentified individuals must be meticulously done since there is usually only one contact with the body. The state of the oral cavity in general and of the dentition and its supporting structures should be noted. The following details should be recorded on a post-mortem dental identification record form (see Figures 34 and 35):

1. <u>Missing teeth</u> - should be marked with an "X" on the dental chart. It is important to determine whether a tooth was lost ante-mortem or post-mortem. A tooth lost post-mortem leaves a clear socket with sharp bone margins around the socket edge. A socket lacking sharp margins and partially filled with bone indicates a tooth lost ante-mortem. A socket completely filled with bone denotes the tooth was lost a considerable time before death (nine months to a year or more).

142

CASE NO. _____
M.E. CASE NO. _____
CITY/COUNTY _____
DATE _____

Circumstances requiring Examination:
_____
_____
_____

Site of Examination:
_____
_____

Outline all caries and restorations on chart. Shade in restorations only. See CODE.

CODE

A   Amalgam Filling
G   Gold Filling
S   Silicate or plastic filling
X   Tooth missing
LPM   Lost tooth post-mortem
PC   Porcelain crown
GC   Gold Crown
SC   Steel crown
VC   Veneer crown
B   Fixed bridge (use brackets beginning and ending with supporting teeth)
PD   Partial Denture
FD   Full Denture

Post-Mortem Dental Photographs   Yes ___ No ___
Post-Mortem Dental X-Rays   Yes ___ No ___

Name and Address of Examiner:
_____
_____
_____

Signature of Examiner:
_____

Name of Investigating Agency:
_____
_____

Investigating Officer :
_____

Jaw Relationship:
__ Normal
__ Protruding Upper Jaw
__ Protruding Lower Jaw

Prosthetic Appliances:
Maxilla:
__ Fixed Bridge
__ Partial Dentures
__ Full Dentures
Mandible:
__ Fixed Bridge
__ Partial Dentures
__ Full Dentures

Describe Prosthetic Applicances:
_____
_____
_____

Abnormalities and other Oral Conditions:
_____
_____

Antemortem Records obtained from:
_____
_____

Describe Antemortem Records:
_____
_____
_____
_____

Additional Notes or Drawings on Back?
__ Yes __ No

THIS BOX TO BE FILLED IN IF IDENTIFICATION IS MADE: Date: _____ Time: _____
Name of Deceased: _____
Address: _____
Birthdate _____ Age _____ Sex _____ Race _____ Physician _____
Death Certificate Information: _____

FIGURE 34. DENTAL IDENTIFICATION CHART AND RECORD FORM.

DENTAL IDENTIFICATION RECORD

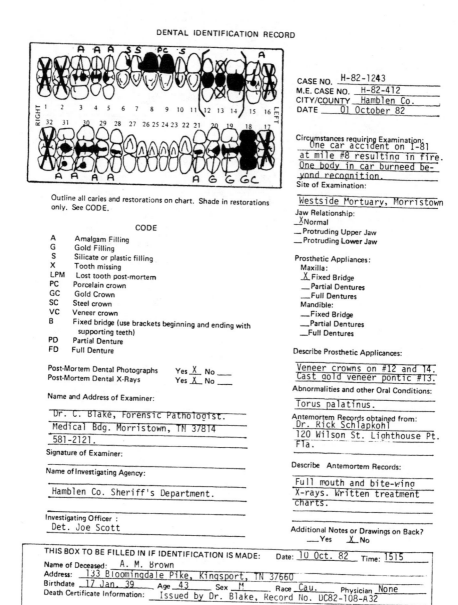

Outline all caries and restorations on chart. Shade in restorations only. See CODE.

CODE

A   Amalgam Filling
G   Gold Filling
S   Silicate or plastic filling
X   Tooth missing
LPM   Lost tooth post-mortem
PC   Porcelain crown
GC   Gold Crown
SC   Steel crown
VC   Veneer crown
B   Fixed bridge (use brackets beginning and ending with supporting teeth)
PD   Partial Denture
FD   Full Denture

Post-Mortem Dental Photographs   Yes _X_ No ___
Post-Mortem Dental X-Rays   Yes _X_ No ___

Name and Address of Examiner:

Dr. C. Blake, Forensic Pathologist.
Medical Bdg. Morristown, TN 37814
581-2121.

Signature of Examiner:

Name of Investigating Agency:

Hamblen Co. Sheriff's Department.

Investigating Officer :
Det. Joe Scott

CASE NO. H-82-1243
M.E. CASE NO. H-82-412
CITY/COUNTY Hamblen Co.
DATE 01 October 82

Circumstances requiring Examination:
One car accident on I-81 at mile #8 resulting in fire. One body in car burneed beyond recognition.
Site of Examination:

Westside Mortuary, Morristown

Jaw Relationship:
_X_ Normal
__ Protruding Upper Jaw
__ Protruding Lower Jaw

Prosthetic Appliances:
Maxilla:
_X_ Fixed Bridge
__ Partial Dentures
__ Full Dentures
Mandible:
__ Fixed Bridge
__ Partial Dentures
__ Full Dentures

Describe Prosthetic Appliances:

Veneer crowns on #12 and 14. Cast gold veneer pontic #13.

Abnormalities and other Oral Conditions:

Torus palatinus.

Antemortem Records obtained from:
Dr. Rick Schlapkohl
120 Wilson St. Lighthouse Pt.
Fla.

Describe Antemortem Records:

Full mouth and bite-wing X-rays. Written treatment charts.

Additional Notes or Drawings on Back?
__ Yes   _X_ No

THIS BOX TO BE FILLED IN IF IDENTIFICATION IS MADE: Date: 10 Oct. 82   Time: 1515
Name of Deceased: A. M. Brown
Address: 133 Bloomingdale Pike, Kingsport, TN 37660
Birthdate 17 Jan. 39   Age 43   Sex M   Race Cau.   Physician None
Death Certificate Information: Issued by Dr. Blake, Record No. DC82-108-A32

FIGURE 35. EXAMPLE OF COMPLETED DENTAL IDENTIFICATION RECORD FORM.

2. <u>Restorations</u> - should be drawn anatomically, showing shape and size on the tooth surface involved. Shading the chart drawing differentiates it from untreated dental caries (tooth decay). To indicate tooth surfaces involved, the following code symbols may be utilized:

> M=Mesial, surface toward the midline
> D=Distal, surface away from the midline
> F=Facial, surface toward the cheek (buccal) or lip (labial)
> L=Lingual, surface toward the tongue
> O=Occlusal, chewing surface of molar and bicuspid teeth
> I=Incisal, biting surface of anterior teeth

When more than one surface is involved, a combination of letters is used, for example:

> MO=Mesial Occlusal surfaces
> DOF=Distal Occlusal Facial surfaces

3. <u>Caries</u> - should be unshaded areas drawn on the dental chart. These areas indicate any decay found on the teeth at the time of the post-mortem examination.

4. <u>Prostheses</u> - any prosthetic appliance (fixed bridgework, partial denture, full dentures, etc.) worn by the deceased at the time of death should be described in detail. Label each dummy tooth (pontics) as a missing tooth with an "X". Draw abutments (inlays, crowns, etc.) anatomically on the dental chart. In some cases a processed identifier giving a name and identifying number, may be found processed into dentures.

5. <u>Occlusal Relationships</u> - may be described as normal, protruding upper jaw, or protruding lower jaw.

6. __Anomalies__ - any unusual conditions of the oral cavity should be recorded and described in detail.

7. __Age Estimation__ - an estimation of the age of the deceased may be made by dental examination. For example, extensive wear on tooth surfaces, excessive bone loss, dentition development, eruption sequence of teeth, cross-sections, etc., may give the forensic odontologist an indication of the age of the deceased person.

Bite Mark Identification

Living individuals associated with criminal activity may be identified by bite-mark evidence. Sexual offenses where persons have been bitten or where criminals have eaten foodstuffs at the scene of a crime may be useful identification evidence. It should be noted that bite-marks are subject to wide variation depending upon how they are produced and the material involved. The interpretation of bite-marks requires extensive experience to determine whether a particular individual was responsible. It is generally easier to use such evidence to exclude a particular person rather than for positive identification of the person who made them. The presence of saliva in and around the bite-mark may also provide associative evidence, particularly if the perpetrator is a secretor whereby the saliva may be bloodtyped.

Bite-marks on human tissues are the result of a physical attack either by an animal or a human. Such marks may be seen in sexual offenses if the bite-mark is human. The morphology of human skin is not a good medium for recording bite marks. Bite-marks on human skin should be measured, photographed, and cast into a model. These procedures must be carried out with the victim in the same position in which the attack occurred due to distortion of tissues which may render inaccurate measurements. It is not recommended to remove tissues (in dead victims) because of distortion caused by the mechanical act of removal and the drying of tissues.

Whereas bite-marks in human skin produce indentations that are not particularly useful for identification, bite-marks in foodstuffs produces a shearing of the teeth providing an excellent medium for identification. Variations of bite-marks in foodstuffs are dependent upon the consistency of the food bitten (i.e., bite marks in cheese provide a better means of identification than an apple). Deterioration of the food will distort the shape of the bite-mark. Therefore, measurements, photography, and casts should be made of bite-marks in foodstuffs as well as human tissues. The procedure for recording bite-marks on foodstuffs and in human tissues by measurement, photography, and casting are similar.

Obtaining Bite-Mark Impressions

Plaster of paris has been used for making casts of bite-marks in skin and foodstuffs. Recently, development in making dental impressions and other casting materials have been utilized with better results (5). A mold is first made of the bite-mark by using plaster, clay, or a plastic dental mold material. The mold is a negative of the bite-mark impression. A cast may be made from the mold to provide a positive image model of the bitemark on the victim. The mold and/or cast may be compared with the suspect's bite impression in wax.

V. Identifying Burned Human Bodies

When death occurs during a fire, the body may be burned beyond recognition. The medical examiner must identify the deceased and establish the cause of death (was death due to fire?). Any remnants of clothing should be removed and

147

preserved. It is possible to identify body fluids from clothing and flooring even when badly burned. Any material retained for laboratory examination should be placed in glass containers and not in plastic bags. Portions of tissues that have been exposed to intense heat for a short period should be removed for laboratory examination. For instance, the blackened skin of the hands may be detached like a pair of gloves.

In most cases, where an individual has been burned beyond visual recognition and where fingerprints cannot be obtained, identification must be made by forensic odontologists and forensic anthropologists.

References

1. Most states forbid the dissection or mutilation of dead human bodies without consent from a court of law.

2. McLaughlin, Jack E. (Ed.), The Detection of Buried Bodies, (Yuba City, California: ANDERMAC), p. 20.

3. Atkins, Leonard and Potsaid, Majie, "Roentgenographic Identification of Human Remains," JAMA, 240:21, 1978.

4. Boyde, A., "Estimation of Age at Death of Young Human Skeletal Remains from Incremental Lines in the Dental Enamel," in Third International Meeting in Forensic Immunology, Medicine, Pathology, and Toxicology, Abridged Proceedings, (Amsterdam: Excerpta Medica Foundation, 1963).

5. Souviron, Richard, et al., "Obtaining the Bitemark Impression (Mold) from Skin," FBI Law Enforcement Bulletin, January 1982, pp. 8-11.

Additional Reading

Bass, William M., and Birkby, Walter H., "Exhumation: The Method Could Make a Difference," FBI Law Enforcement Bulletin, July 1978.

Imaizumi, Masataka, "Locating Buried Bodies," FBI Law Enforcement Bulletin, August 1974.

Luntz, Lester L., Handbook for Dental Identification, (Philadelphia: J.B. Lippincott Co., 1973).

McLaughlin, Jack (Ed.), The Detection of Buried Bodies, (Yuba City, California: ANDERMAC).

O'Hara, Charles E., Fundamentals of Criminal Investigation, 5th Edition, (Springfield, Illinois: Charles C. Thomas, 1980).

O'Hara, Charles E., and Osterburg, James W., An Introduction to Criminalistics, (Bloomington, Indiana: Indiana University Press, 1972).

Sperber, Norman D., "Trial Aids and the Role of the Forensic Odontologist," FBI Law Enforcement Bulletin, March 1975.

Ubelaker, Douglas H., Human Skeletal Remains: Excavation, Analysis, Interpretation, (Chicago: Aldine Publishing Co., 1978).

U.S. Department of Justice, Crime Scene Search and Physical Evidence Handbook, (Washington, D.C.: Law Enforcement Assistance Administration, 1973).

8

IDENTIFYING HUMAN SKELETAL REMAINS

The last link in the chain of human identification lies with forensic anthropology. Forensic anthropology adapts the principles of anthropology to medicine and law. Anthropologists are concerned with the study of man from the earliest periods of time. Physical anthropologists have studied the physical characteristics of man for decades and have developed extensive research in the identification of human skeletal material. When an unknown human subject has decomposed or been burned beyond recognition, it may be necessary to consult a forensic anthropologist to determine the identity of the individual.

I. OSTEOLOGY

Osteology is the study of skeletal structures and bones (Figures 36, 37, 38, and 39). It is necessary that law enforcement individuals be somewhat knowledgeable of this field when confronted with identifying human skeletal remains. It is not uncommon for citizens to walk into a police station with a bone and ask a police officer: "Is this a human bone?" Pets and other animals have been known to carry home portions of bones from decomposed remains of animals and humans. Most individuals do not know the differences between human and animal bones. However, there are many cases where police officers have discarded human bones in the trash believing they were only animal bones. In many instances, only an expert can make the determination if a bone is human or animal. If a bone or portions of a skeleton are suspected to be human, they should be examined by a physical anthropologist or other medical expert for a positive determination. If the bones are determined to be human, the law enforcement officer must then investigate. The next step

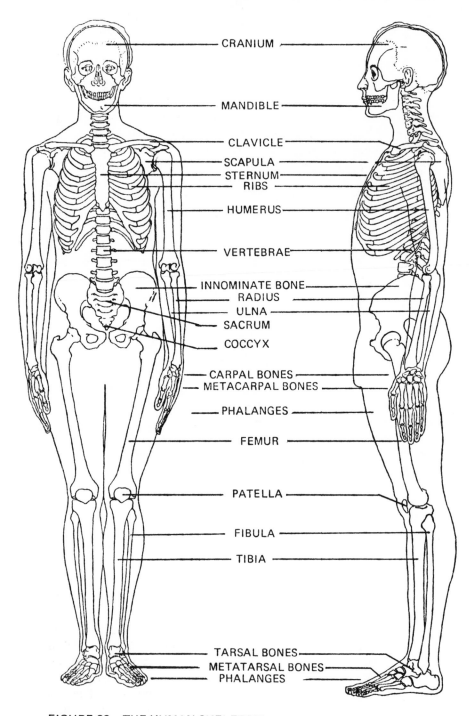

CRANIUM

MANDIBLE

CLAVICLE
SCAPULA
STERNUM
RIBS

HUMERUS

VERTEBRAE

INNOMINATE BONE
RADIUS
ULNA
SACRUM
COCCYX

CARPAL BONES
METACARPAL BONES

PHALANGES

FEMUR

PATELLA

FIBULA

TIBIA

TARSAL BONES
METATARSAL BONES
PHALANGES

FIGURE 36.   THE HUMAN SKELETON.

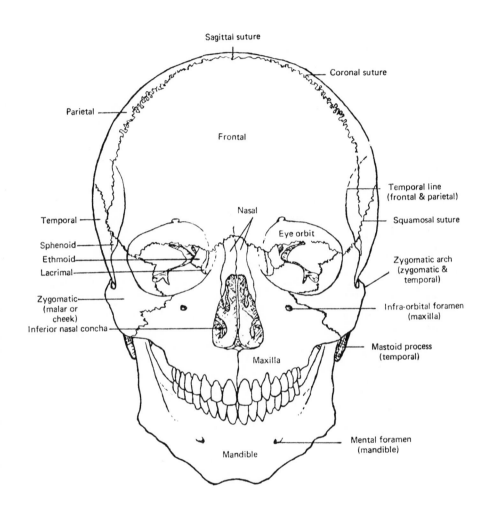

Sagittal suture

Coronal suture

Parietal

Frontal

Temporal line
(frontal & parietal)

Nasal

Eye orbit

Squamosal suture

Temporal

Sphenoid

Ethmoid

Lacrimal

Zygomatic arch
(zygomatic &
temporal)

Zygomatic
(malar or
cheek)

Infra-orbital foramen
(maxilla)

Inferior nasal concha

Maxilla

Mastoid process
(temporal)

Mental foramen
(mandible)

Mandible

FIGURE 37. BONES AND PARTS OF THE SKULL — FRONT VIEW.

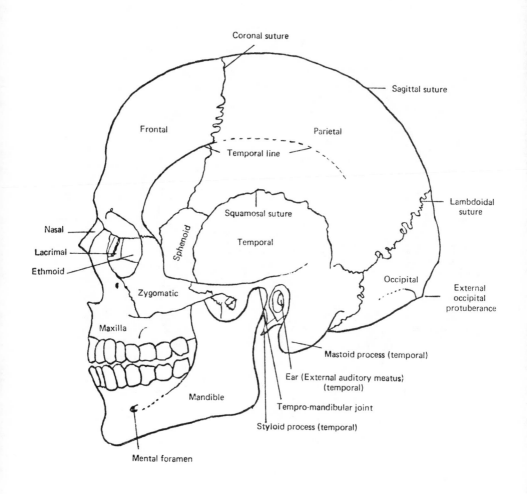

FIGURE 38. BONES AND PARTS OF THE SKULL — SIDE VIEW.

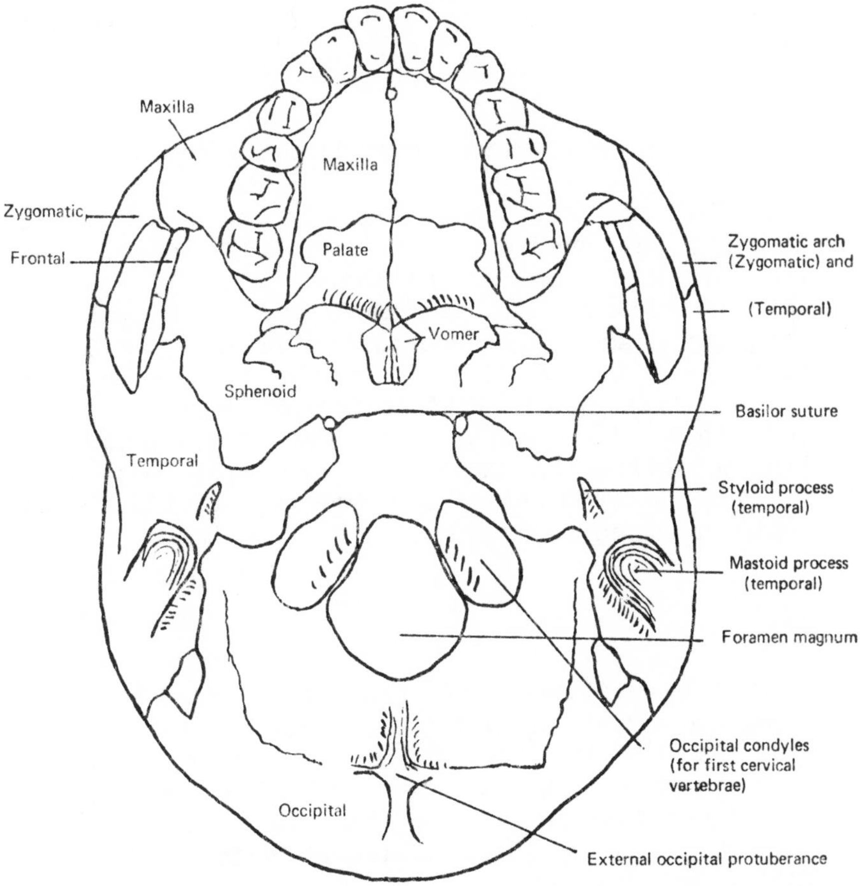
Maxilla
Maxilla
Zygomatic
Frontal
Palate
Vomer
Sphenoid
Temporal
Occipital
Zygomatic arch
(Zygomatic) and
(Temporal)
Basilor suture
Styloid process
(temporal)
Mastoid process
(temporal)
Foramen magnum
Occipital condyles
(for first cervical
vertebrae)
External occipital protuberance

FIGURE 39. BONES AND PARTS OF THE SKULL – BASE VIEW.

involves locating where the bones were discovered. This may prove difficult if a pet or other animal has carried the bone from another location. Forensic anthropologists may be able to help locate the remaining skeleton if this is the case. Once a human skeleton is located, a forensic anthropologist should be requested to examine the remains in order to provide partial identification.

II. Identifying Human Skeletal Remains

The questions that can be answered by a forensic anthropologist include: 1) age of the individual; 2) sex of the individual; 3) race of the individual; 4) how tall the individual was (stature); and 5) handedness (right- or left-handed). In addition, forensic anthropologists may determine previous injuries to bone structure and anomalies in bone structures that may aid in the identification process. In some cases, a forensic anthropologist may reconstruct the facial features of an unknown skull.

<u>Age</u>

Two questions are generally asked of the forensic anthropologist with respect to age: 1) How old was the individual when death occurred; and 2) How long has the individual been dead. The determination of how long the individual has been dead is the most difficult determination as has been discussed in Chapter 6. There are, however, certain areas and characteristics on a human skeleton that may be examined to determine the age of the individual when he or she died. Some of the more accurate methods are described below:

SUBADULT:

1.   <u>Dentition:</u> Man is a mammal and as such has two sets of teeth, a Deciduous (baby or

milk) set which appear between 6 and 24 months and are replaced by Adult teeth between 6 1/2 and 11 1/2 years. The 20 Deciduous teeth usually erupt around 6 months and are all erupted by 24 months. Deciduous teeth can be distinguished from adult teeth because they are:

    a. Smaller in size.
    b. More yellow in color (because the enamel covering the dentine is thinner than in adult teeth).

Usually all Deciduous teeth have erupted by 24 months (2 years). We retain this set of teeth until approximately 6 1/2 years when they begin to be replaced by adult teeth.

2. <u>Epiphyses</u>: During the period of body growth the ends of long bones will have epiphyses. Epiphyses allow room for the bone to grow at both ends. The epiphysis is preformed in cartilage which will calcify (ossify) into bone as growth proceeds. Bones will ossify at epiphyseal sites in various stages of life so that an age bracket may be estimated. For instance, the last epiphysis to unite and ossify is the sternal end of the clavicle at about age 25. Epiphyses are an excellent method of estimating the age of a young individual (Figure 40).

ADULT:

1. <u>Pubic Symphysis</u>: The pubic region of the pelvis, where the two innominate bones come together, is another area on the skeleton that age may be estimated. Younger adults have rougher surface area at the pubic symphysis than older individuals. The older an individual becomes, the smoother the surface between the two innominate bones (see Figure 41). A forensic anthropologist can assess the degree of change to the pubic symphysis and estimate an age at death from

157

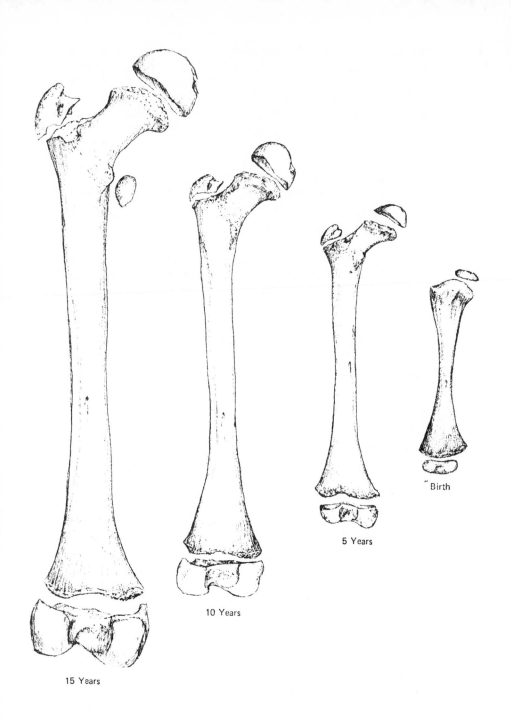

15 Years

10 Years

5 Years

Birth

FIGURE 40. EPIPHYSES OF THE FEMUR.

158

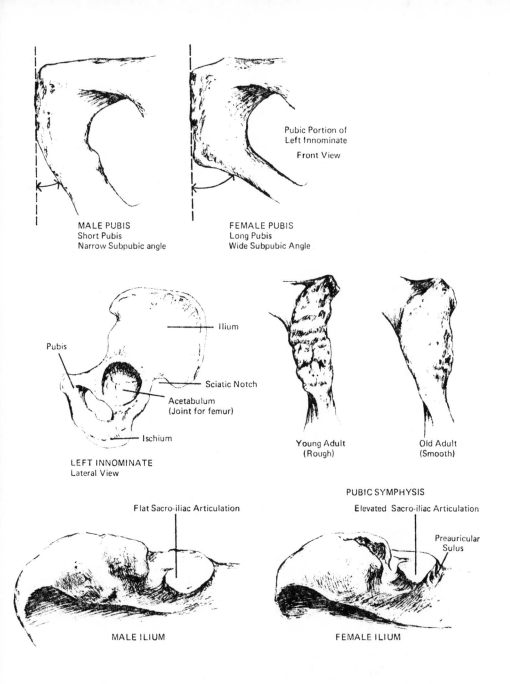

MALE PUBIS
Short Pubis
Narrow Subpubic angle

FEMALE PUBIS
Long Pubis
Wide Subpubic Angle

Pubic Portion of
Left Innominate

Front View

Ilium

Pubis

Sciatic Notch

Acetabulum
(Joint for femur)

Ischium

LEFT INNOMINATE
Lateral View

Young Adult
(Rough)

Old Adult
(Smooth)

PUBIC SYMPHYSIS

Flat Sacro-iliac Articulation

Elevated Sacro-iliac Articulation

Preauricular
Sulus

MALE ILIUM

FEMALE ILIUM

FIGURE 41.   AGE AND SEX DETERMINATION FROM THE PUBIC REGION.

159

standards established for both males and females.

2. <u>Adult Teeth:</u> The first adult teeth to erupt are the First or 6 year molars. These appear behind the Deciduous molars. Around 6 1/2 years the Deciduous Incisor teeth are replaced by the adult Incisors. Usually all of the Deciduous teeth have been replaced by adult teeth by 11 1/2 years. The Second adult molar erupts at age 12 and the Third molar (a genetically very unstable tooth) may or may not erupt at age 18.

3. <u>Osteon Counting:</u> Osteon counting could be compared to the counting of rings of a cross-sectioned tree to determine age. A cross-section near the middle of a bone (usually the femur) is obtained and examined under a microscope. The inside of bones are made up of canals (osteons) which carry nutrients to the bone. Osteons live and die and are replaced by other osteons cutting into the bone. The older an individual is, the more osteons he/she will have. Osteons are one reason why older individuals have "brittle bones."

4. <u>Osteo-Arthritic Characteristics:</u> Osteo-arthritis is a build up of bone around the surfaces of skeletal joints. Joints begin to wear out as an individual becomes older. As joints wear out, the lining of bone becomes inflammed and a build up of bone may begin. The spine may indicate arthritic lipping (spurs on the spine) which may give an indication of age.

5. <u>Faveolae Granulares (Pacchionian Pits):</u> Faveolae granulares are small pits on the internal surface of the skull that appear as opaque patches when using transmitted light. Faveolae granulares may appear in the skull after an individual has reached his/her 60th birthday. Faveolae granulares are also known

160

as pacchionian pits and usually appear lateral to the midline of the skull on the inner surface.

Sex

The sex of a skeleton may be determined from the pelvis region, skull, and general skeletal size. It is difficult to determine the sex of a skeleton if puberty has not been reached. In a complete adult skeleton, sex can be determined in about 96 percent of the cases (1).

The most accurate area for sex determination of an adult skeleton is the pelvis region. Females have broader hips than males. The length of the pubic bone in females is longer than in males. Females have a broader sciatic notch than males. On the sacro-iliac joint of females there is a ridge of bone that is absent on males (see Figures 41 and 42).

The adult skull may also indicate the sex of an individual. Males usually have larger and more rugged skulls than females. Males have heavier supraorbital ridges, and larger and longer mastoid processes than females. Heavier muscle markings on the back of male skulls is quite common, whereas females usually have shallow muscle markings on the back of the skull. Males have larger mouths than females. The male chin (mandible) is usually blunter, broader, and more square than on the female. Female chins are usually narrow and come to a point at the midline.

The general size of "sexual" dimorphism of an adult skeleton should give an indication of sex. Male skeletons are usually larger than female skeletons (because they grow approximately two years longer than females). The head portion of the adult humerus and femur may also give an indication to the sex of the adult skeleton. The diameter of the head of the humerus and femur rarely exceds 43 mm in females.

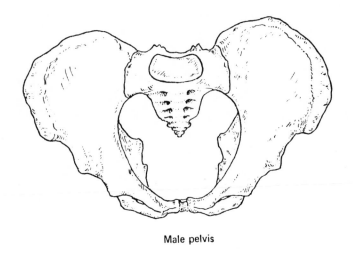

Male pelvis

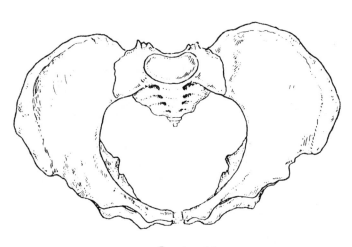

Female pelvis

FIGURE 42.   SEX COMPARISON OF HUMAN PELVIS.

Race

There are three major social groups of man: 1) Caucasoid (white); 2) Negroid (black); and 3) Mongoloid (red or yellow). The only accurate area on the skeleton that race can be determined is the skull. Caucasoids are characterized by a pointed face whereas negroids and mongoloids have rounded, flatter faces. Negroid individuals are characterized by alveolar prognathism (protrusion of the mouth region). In addition, negroid individuals usually lack a ridge of bone (sill) at the base of the nasal opening that is common among caucasoid individuals. Negroid skulls often have an ivory texture because the bone is more dense than in the other races. The eye-orbits in mongoloid and negroid skulls are usually rounder in shape than caucasoids.

Dentition may also give an indication of race. Mongoloids usually have "shovel-shaped" incisors and they often come together on the occlusal surface (biting edge) in the incisor region. Caucasoids have non-shovel incisors with a slight overbite. In some cases, scalp hair may be found on the skull which may give an indication for race. Birds will sometimes use human head hair from decaying bodies to build nests during the spring and summer. Care should be taken to check bird nests in the area of a decaying body for evidence of hair.

Stature

Forensic anthropologists can estimate the living height of an unknown person by examining any of the long bones in the skeleton. The femur is the most accurate bone for determination of height (2). The maximum length of the femur is measured in centimeters and is used in the following formula:

2.32 (length of femur) + 65.53 ± 3.94.

Because of the range of variability among the human population, the ± 3.94 is utilized in the formula in order to bracket the stature estimations. For example, if a femur of an unknown individual measures 45.0 centimeters in length: 2.32 (45.0) + 65.53 ± 3.94 = 165.99 to 173.87 cm or 5'4 1/2" to 5'7" in height. When both femurs are available, a better estimation of height can be made.

Handedness

Approximately 85 percent of the population is right handed. The preferred side of the body receives more blood supply; thus, stronger muscles, longer bones, and better development occurs. Forensic anthropologists may be able to determine the handedness of an unknown individual by examining the bones to determine which side is "preferred".

III. Facial Reconstruction

In some cases a positive identification can only be achieved by facial reconstruction. Facial reconstruction involves the rebuilding of tissue thickness over the skull. Physical anthropologists have utilized this technique with skeletal remains of pre-historic man. Forensic anthropologists utilize the same techniques in order to produce a likeness of an individual for identification purposes. There are several methods of facial reconstruction available to anthropologists. Reconstruction by photographs, reconstruction by composite drawings, and reconstruction by clay are three methods commonly employed.

Photographic reconstruction requires a photograph of the suspected missing individual. A photograph of the unidentified skull is made in the same angle as the photograph of the missing person. The two photographs are enlarged and superimposed to determine a "fit." This method is excellent for excluding individuals; that is, one may show that the two photographs are not of the same person. This is a difficult method for positive identification, however. There are also problems associated with the photograph of the missing person for comparative purposes. In many cases, a recent, quality photograph (or portrait) of the missing person is not available. In addition, it is difficult to obtain accurate measurements for comparison. The use of two television cameras for superimposing the images on a single display screen may help.

Artist composites for facial reconstruction of human skulls have been successfully performed. Scale photographs (front and side views) are made of the unknown skull. A composite artist is utilized to sketch a face over the skull with assistance from a physical anthropologist. It is necessary that the artist remain within known anthropological limits; particularly tissue depths, placement of the eyes, ears, mouth, and nose. Once a sketch of the unknown person has been completed, it may be circulated by law enforcement agencies and news media for identification purposes.

Clay reconstruction is one of the most accurate methods of facial reconstruction. The procedure includes the rebuilding in clay of skin and facial features on the unknown skull. Anthropologists have extensively studied skin depth for different races of man. Skin depth markers are placed on the skull in the appropriate points and clay strips are used to connect the markers. Clay is then filled in to create the face.

The procedure for any facial reconstruction involves 1) determination of age; 2) determination of sex; and 3) determination of race. In addition, weight of the subject may be estimated by the size of the clothing remaining at the time of discovery. Hair length and color may be determined by recovering hairs of the victim at the scene. The color of eyes and shape of the ears, and sometimes, nose are disadvantages of the procedure. It is impossible to determine eye color from skeletal remains. It is also impossible to determine the shape of the ears, and, sometimes, the shape of the nose from skeletal remains.

IV. Role Of The Police Investigator In Skeletal Identification

If skeletal remains are discovered, identification will require the expertise of a forensic anthropologist. Forensic anthropologists are capable of providing useful information from skeletal remains of individuals. Sex, race, age, stature, body build, nutritional history, previous injuries and anomalies, pregnancies, and even occupation may be determined from an anthropological examination of skeletal remains. It is important that investigators at the scene of the discovery of a human skeleton collect as much evidence as possible (i.e., hair, clothing, jewelry, etc.), as well as bones to help the forensic anthropologist determine identity.

The investigating police officer should treat the removal of skeletal remains the same as any crime scene search. In addition to notifying the coroner/medical examiner, the investigator should notify a forensic anthropologist. It is recommended that the forensic anthropologist be summoned to the scene as well as the medical examiner.

Most states have at least one forensic anthropologist available for criminal investigations. Forensic anthropologists

166

generally possess a Doctor of Philosophy degree in physical anthropology rather than a Doctor of Medicine degree. Therefore, when human skeletal remains are located it may be necessary to notify the proper medical personnel (e.g., medical examiner) to provide legal authority for anthropological examinations.

References

1. Krogman, W.M., The Human Skeleton in Forensic Medicine, (Springfield, Illinois: Charles C. Thomas, 1962).

2. Bass, William M., Human Osteology: A Laboratory and Field Manual of the Human Skeleton, 2nd Edition, (Columbia, Missouri: Missouri Archaeological Society, 1971), p. 175.

Additional Reading

Angel, Lawrence J., "Bones Can Fool People," FBI Law Enforcement Bulletin, January, 1974.

Atkins, L., and Majic, P., "Roentgenographic Identification of Human Remains," JAMA, November, 1978.

Bass, William M., Human Osteology: A Laboratory and Field Manual of the Human Skeleton, 2nd Edition, (Columbia, Missouri: Missouri Archaeological Society, 1971).

Cherry, Donald G. and Angel, Lawrence J., "Personality Reconstruction from Unidentified Remains," FBI Law Enforcement Bulletin, August, 1977.

Krogman, W.M., "The Reconstruction of the Living
    Head from the Skull," FBI Law Enforcement
    Bulletin, July - August, 1943.

Krogman, W.M., The Human Skeleton in Forensic
    Medicine, (Springfield, Illinois: Charles
    C. Thomas, 1962).

Stewart, T.D., "What the Bones Tell - Today," FBI
    Law Enforcement Bulletin, February, 1972.

9

LEGAL ISSUES IN HUMAN IDENTIFICATION

I. Rules Of Evidence

Law enforcement practitioners and forensic scientists are subject to the rules of evidence as applied to the courts of the United States. A failure to conform to the rules of evidence may result in the exclusion of any evidence presented to a court of law. The rules of evidence were developed to prevent untrustworthy, illegal, or biased evidence to be presented to court juries. Members of a court jury are usually lay individuals who have little knowledge of legal procedures or the facts of a case presented to them. In addition, it is obviously necessary for the courts to establish rules to carry on court proceedings in an orderly and efficient manner. Evidentiary rules have been developed and formulated by the courts and by legislative action in order to meet these objectives.

II. Types Of Evidence

Evidence has been defined as the means utilized to prove an unknown or disputed fact. Evidence is information on which an individual may base a decision. Evidence presented in a court of law is known as legal evidence. Legal evidence is:

> any species of proof, or probative matter, legally presented at the trial of an issue, by the act of the parties and through the medium of witnesses, records, documents, concrete objects, etc., for the purpose of inducing belief in the minds of the court or jury as to their contention (1).

In other words, legal evidence means "that which demonstrates or makes clear or ascertains the truth of the very fact or point in issue, either on one side or the other (2)."

169

There are many forms of legal evidence. Among the forms of importance to human evidence include:

Direct Evidence: that means of proof which tends to show the existence of a fact in question, without the intervention of the proof of any other fact (1). For instance, if a witness testified that he saw a particular individual commit an act, this would be direct evidence.

Circumstantial Evidence: means that the existence of a principle fact is only inferred from the circumstances. The truth is arrived at through entrances of probabilities arising from an association of facts (3). For instance, a crime lab technician may testify that the blood on an accused's clothing was of the same type of blood as the deceased's. Blood typing is circumstantial evidence because factors of probability exist.

Testimonial Evidence: evidence which come through witnesses speaking under oath or affirmation before a court of law. The witness giving testimony must be competent. The courts determine whether a witness' testimony is competent or not before that testimony is presented before a jury. For instance, an expert witness must show to the court that he/she is, in fact, an expert on a particular subject before he/she is allowed to present his/her opinions before a jury.

Documentary Evidence: documents, records, photographs, and writings which are not objectionable under the exclusionary rules of evidence. Suicide notes, medical examiner reports, and identification photographs are all documentary evidence.

Real Evidence: or "physical evidence" is "things themselves, on view or inspection, as distinguished from the description of them by the mouth of the witness (1)." For instance, an

170

expert witness on fingerprints may testify that a latent fingerprint (real evidence) found at a crime scene matches the inked fingerprint of an individual.

Proof: is the effect of evidence or the establishment of fact by evidence. In U.S. criminal courts, "proof beyond a reasonable doubt" is required for a decision made by the court or jury to convict a defendant.

III. Identification Of The Living

The legal issues surrounding the identification of living individuals is primarily directed at identifying individuals involved in criminal offenses. Generally, no person in the United States has a right to refuse his/her identification. The courts have held that processes involved in the identification of an individual (e.g., fingerprints, photographs, voice-prints, line-ups, blood, etc.) do not violate an individual's constitutional rights. Challenges to identification procedures have been made that suggest such procedures violate the Fourth, Fifth, Sixth, and Fourteenth Amendments of the U.S. Constitution. The Fourth Amendment of the U.S. Constitution states:

> The right of the people to be secure in their persons, houses, papers, and effects, against unreasonable searches and seizures, shall not be violated, and no warrants shall issue, but upon probable cause, supported by oath or affirmation, and particularly describing the place to be searched, and the persons or things to be seized.

The Fifth Amendment of the U.S. Constitution states:

> No person shall . . . be compelled in any criminal case to be a witness against himself.

171

The Sixth Amendment of the U.S. Constitution states:

> In all criminal prosecutions, the accused shall enjoy the right to . . have the Assistance of Counsel for his defense.

The Fourteenth Amendment of the U.S. Constitution states:

> No state shall make or enforce any law which shall abridge the privileges or immunities of citizens of the United States; nor shall any State deprive any person of life, liberty, or property, without due process of law; nor deny to any person within its jurisdiction the equal protection of the laws.

Fingerprints, photographs, line-ups, dental examinations, and evidence obtained from the body of an accused, have all been challenged under one or more of the four U.S. Constitution Amendments mentioned above.

Fingerprints and Photographs

The challenges to fingerprints and photographs for identification purposes have indicated that a suspect incriminates himself in violation of the Fifth Amendment. One early U.S. Supreme Court case, Holt v. U.S., distinguished between a person compelled to give verbal evidence and requiring him to have all his fingerprints taken (4). In Schmerber v. California, the U.S. Supreme Court stated:

> We hold that the privilege [self-incrimination] protects an accused only from being compelled to testify against himself or otherwise provide the State with evidence of a testimonial or communicative nature. It [the self-incrimination privilege] offers no protection against compulsion to submit to

fingerprinting, photographing, or measurements, to write or speak for identification, to appear in court, to stand, to assume a stance, to walk, or to make a particular gesture (5).

As a general rule, a suspect should be under a legal arrest before identification procedures are undertaken. If no arrest has been made, an individual may give permission or a court order or a search warrant may be obtained in order for identification processes to be made. Of particular importance is the fingerprinting and photographing of juveniles. In most states, a court order from the Juvenile Court is required before legal processing of any juvenile's fingerprints or photographs.

Line-Ups

Challenges to line-ups have been made with respect to violations of self-incrimination (Fifth Amendment), right to counsel (Sixth Amendment), and due process (Fourteenth Amendment).

The U.S. Supreme Court held, in United States v. Wade, that compelling the accused merely to exhibit his person for observation prior to trial, "involves no compulsion of the accused to give evidence having testimonial significance (6)." The courts have been consistent in holding that the mere viewing of a suspect by an eyewitness does not violate the self-incrimination privilege because the suspect is not required to be an unwilling witness against himself.

The question of the right to counsel was considered by the U.S. Supreme Court in the Kirby v. Illinois case. The Court stated:

The initiation of judicial criminal proceedings is far from a mere formalism. It is the starting point of our whole system of adversary criminal justice. For it is only then that the government has committed itself to prosecute, and only then that the adverse positions of government and defendant have solidified. . . It is this point, therefore, that makes the commencement of the "criminal prosecutions" to which alone the explicit guarantees of the Sixth Amendment are applicable (7).

Generally, counsel is not required at the scene of an arrest, where the police officer is merely trying to determine whether he/she has the right suspect. However, identification procedures may be a violation of the Sixth Amendment if the procedure is so suggestive as to be biased toward the defendant. The courts hold that a suspect may have the right to counsel at identification proceedings to make certain that the procedure is a fair and unbiased one for the accused.

If a line-up is suggestive to the point that mistaken identity could result, the procedure violates due process. For example, if a person is placed in a six person line-up with five other persons of a different race, this would obviously make the procedure unfair. In a U.S. Supreme Court decision, Foster v. California, line-ups or other confrontation for identification must not be suggestive (8). Another U.S. Supreme Court case, Neil v. Biggers, explained that the primary evil to be avoided is the likelihood of mistaken identity or misidentification (9). The Court considered five factors dealing with misidentification: 1) the witness' degree of attention; 2) the witness' opportunity to view the criminal during the crime; 3) the accuracy of the witness' prior description of the criminal; 4) the level of certainty demonstrated by the witness at the line-up or confrontation; and 5) the length of time between the crime and the confrontation (9).

Photographic (mug-shot) line-ups are frequently used by law enforcement agencies. Photographs used in a line-up must follow the same due process rules as in live confrontations. Although photographs are not governed by the self-incrimination or right to counsel clauses of the Fifth and Sixth Amendments, they are governed by due process. Photographs, as in live subjects, may not be so suggestive as to create a misidentification. It is recommended that photographs or mug-shots of individuals that are to be used in a photographic line-up be similar in appearance, shading, size, and color (10).

Dental Examinations

A United States District Court for Eastern Pennsylvania concluded that self-incrimination protection of the Fifth Amendment was not violated when the suspect was required to have a dental examination for identification purposes (11).

Voice Prints

Voice spectrographic evidence was considered by the U.S. Supreme Court in the case of United States v. Dionisio (12). The Court ruled that compelling a suspect to give voice exemplars for identification purposes did not violate the Fifth Amendment.

Handwriting

Obtaining handwriting exemplars from suspects was considered in two U.S. Supreme Court cases. The case of Gilbert v. California upheld that the taking of handwriting exemplars was reasonable before the appointment of legal counsel (13). In the case of United States v. Mara, the U.S. Supreme Court ruled that taking handwriting exemplars did not constitute an unreasonable search and seizure of a person and, hence, was not in violation of the Fourth Amendment (14).

Body Examinations

Generally, it is not a violation of the Fifth Amendment to examine a suspect's body for traces of blood (15), or to take penis scrapings and saliva samples from a suspect (16). Furthermore, hair samples, fingernail snippings/scrapings, blood samples, or other body extracted evidence is not considered to be a violation of the self-incrimination provisions. However, there is a possibility that Fourth Amendment violations to unreasonable searches and seizures may be challenged if the suspect is not under a legal arrest or if there is no court order or search warrant justifying the search and seizure.

IV. Identification Of The Deceased

Generally, most laws regulating dead body identification and disposition rest with the states. Federal laws deal mainly with interstate transportation of deceased individuals and disposition of dead federal employee's bodies (i.e., military, federal office holders, etc.). Most states have legislated regulations and laws governing the disposition of dead bodies. Generally, any death not attended by a physician (i.e., home or residence deaths and unnatural or accidental deaths) must have a physician and/or coroner examine the body at the scene to confirm and pronounce death. A Certificate of Death is issued by a physician who has attended the victim in the past or by a medical examiner following an autopsy. In some states, the physician who issues a death certificate need not examine the body after death provided that the death is natural and the physician has attended the patient during the near past. However, in suspicious and unnatural deaths, an autopsy is required by law in most states before a death certificate is issued.

Of particular importance to legal matters is the "suspicious death". Coroners and/or medical examiners and law enforcement officials must generally be able to justify detailed examinations of a dead body before a judicial or legislative court. There have been cases where an attending physician has ruled death by natural causes in suspected homicide cases. Many family physicians are also reluctant to rule suicide as a cause of death and indicate accidental death on death certificates. Authority to autopsy a body under these conditions are best dealt with by a court to avoid civil liability suits.

In cases where a deceased individual cannot be identified, an autopsy is usually required by law. In some cases, a dead body may be so severely burned or decomposed as to require the removal of the hands, feet, or even the skeletal frame from the tissue so that a laboratory examination may be made. It is recommended that a court order be obtained for the purpose of such examinations prior to the process to prevent any violation of state criminal or civil codes.

Any unauthorized autopsy is a tort (civil wrong) and the offending party is subject to civil suit for damages. In some cases, an unauthorized autopsy may be considered criminal (i.e., mutilation of dead body laws). Authorization for any autopsy may be made by the consent of the person entitled to custody of the deceased, by the coroner or medical examiner, by the will of the deceased, or by a court order. Because the dead have no right to privacy, the liability for an unauthorized autopsy is dependent upon the sensibilities of the person entitled to custody. Although information from an autopsy is not considered privileged, an unauthorized audience to an autopsy or unauthorized use of photographs may constitute grounds for civil damage claims. A dead body is not considered to be property and a person cannot own a dead body or acquire a title to a dead body. However, because duty of burial falls on the next of kin, the custody of the body is given to that person. Interference with the rights of custody and burial of a dead body may result in a civil suit for mental pain and

suffering.   The   regulations   governing   the
embalming,   intrastate   transportation,   and
interment of a dead body are controlled by the
individual state departments of public health.

When an exhumation or disinterment of a known
dead body from a tomb is requested, authorization
must be given by a court order, coroner, or
district attorney in most states.   Exhumed body
autopsy examinations are never as satisfactory as
a primary autopsy.   In most cases, the body has
been embalmed which interferes with chemical and
toxicological evaluations.   In most states, a
court order authorizing reburial must be obtained
before re-interment of an exhumed body.

References

1.   Black's Law Dictionary, (New York: West
           Publishing Co., 1951).

2.   Leonard v. State, 127 N.E. 464 (1919).

3.   Twin City Fire Insurance Co. v. Lonas, 75
           S.W. (2d) 348 (1934).

4.   Holt v. United States, 218 U.S. 245,   54 L.
           Ed. 1021, 31 S. Ct. 2 (1910).

5.   Schmerber v. California, 384 U.S. 757, 16
           L.Ed. (2d) 908, 86 S.Ct. 1826 (1966).

6.   United States v. Wade, 388 U.S. 218,   18
           L.Ed. (2d) 1149, 87 S.Ct. 1926 (1967).

7.   Kirby v. Illinois, 406 U.S. 682, 32   L.Ed.
           (2d) 411, 92 S.Ct. 1877 (1972).

8.   Foster v. California, 394 U.S. 440,   22
           L.Ed. (2d) 402, 89 S.Ct. 1127 (1969).

9.   Neil v. Biggers, 409 U.S. 188, 34   L.Ed.
           (2d) 401, 93 S.Ct. 375 (1972).

10. Simmons v. United States, 390 U.S. 377, 19 L.Ed. (2d) 1247, 88 S.Ct. 967 (1968).

11. United States v. Holland, 378 F. Supp. 144 (E.D. Pa. 1974).

12. United States v. Dionisio, 410 U.S. 1, 35 L.Ed. (2d) 67, 93 S.Ct. 964 (1973).

13. Gilbert v. California, 388 U.S. 263 (1967)

14. United States v. Mara, 410 U.S. 19 (1973).

15. McFarland v. United States, 150 F. 2d 593 (D.C. Cir. 1945).

16. Brent v. White, 276 F. Supp. 386 (E.D. La. 1967).

Additional Reading

Carlson, Ronald L., Criminal Justice Procedure, 2d Edition, (Cincinnatti: Anderson Publishing Co. 1978).

Dowling, Jerry L., Teaching Materials on Criminal Procedure, (St. Paul, Minnesota: West Publishing Co., 1976).

Klotter, John C. and Kanovitz, Jacqueline, R., Constitutional Law for Police, (Cincinnatti: Anderson Publishing Co., 1977).

Miller, Frank W., et al., Cases and Materials on Criminal Justice Administration, 2d Edition, (New York: The Foundation Press, Inc., 1982).

Stuckey, Gilbert B., Evidence for the Law Enforcement Officer, 3rd Edition, (New York: McGraw-Hill Book Co., 1979).

Waddington, Lawrence C., Criminal Evidence, (Encino, California: Glencoe Publishing Co., Inc., 1978).

INDEX

I

Iannarelli, Alfred, 91
Iannarelli System of Ear Identification, 91
Identi-Kit (see Composite Drawings)
Infrared film (see also Photography), 127
Inked fingerprints, 28
    classification of, 34-47
    taking of, 28
Insect attack, on dead bodies, 117
Iodine fuming, in fingerprints, 26

J

K

Kastle-Meyer test, 55
Keratin Protein, in hair, 73
Kersta, L.G., 94
Kirby v. Illinois, 173

L

Laser light, in fingerprints, 25
Latent fingerprints, 24
    development of, 25
    identification of, 25
Lectins, 50
Leuco-Malachite Test, 54
Light
    infrared, 127, 129, 136
    ultraviolet, 65, 67, 128
Line-ups, 173
    for identification, 173
    legal issues in, 173
Livor Mortis, 112
Lombroso, Cesare, 3
Loops, in fingerprints, 30
Luminol test, 55

M

Medical examiner, 111, 117, 119
Medulla, 74

Skeleton, 151-168
    identification of human, 151-168
    parts of human, 151-156
Skin slippage, 116
Skull, 153
    identification of human, 153
    parts of human, 153-155
Sole prints, 30
Somatic origin, of hair, 76-80
Species, blood determination, 57-59
Spectrograph, voiceprint, 93
Spectrophotometry, infrared, 56
States of human hair growth, 74
Stains, body fluids
    collection of, 67
    identification of, 67
Statistical probability, 2, 82
Stature estimation, in skeletal material, 163
Suspicious death, 124, 176

T
Takayama test, 56
Teeth, 139, 156
    adult human, 139
    children human, 140
Teichmann test, 56
Tented arch, in fingerprints, 36
Tetramethylbenzidine, for blood, 55
Testimonial evidence, 170
Time of death, 111
Trace metal detection, 127
Type lines, in fingerprints, 39

U
Ulnar loops, in fingerprints, 36
Ultraviolet illumination, 65, 67
Urine, 49, 69, 111
U.S. Constitution, 171
U.S. V. Dionisio, 175
U.S. v. Mara, 175
U.S. v. Wade, 173

V

Vaginal stains, 66
Visual searches, 135
Voiceprint evidence, 93
Voiceprint spectrograph, 94

W

Wagenaar test, 56
Will West - William West case, 4
Whorl tracing, in fingerprints, 39
Whorls, in fingerprints, 30

X

X-rays (see radiographs)

Y

Z

Zaner-Bloser Handwriting System, 97

ABOUT THE AUTHORS

Larry S. Miller, Ph.D., is an Assistant Professor with the Department of Criminal Justice at East Tennessee State University, Johnson City, Tennessee. He is former Director of the Walters State Crime Laboratory, Morristown, Tennessee.

William M. Bass, Ph.D., is Professor and Head of Physical Anthropology at the University of Tennessee, Knoxville, and Forensic Anthropologist for the State of Tennessee.

Ramona L. Miller, Ph.D., is Quality Assurance Coordinator for the Helen Ross McNabb Mental Health Center, Knoxville, Tennessee. Dr. Miller previously worked for the Knoxville Police Department. Dr. Miller is also an adjunct Assistant Professor of Public Health and Safety at the University of Tennessee, Knoxville and Department of Criminal Justice at East Tennessee State University, Johnson City.